Linda,
God bless you,
Mary Glynn

DEPRESSION: A WAY OUT

A Christian P...

DEPRESSION:
A Way Out

A Christian Biblical View

Dr. Sam Peeples

THE SHEEP SHOPPE
P.O. BOX 531147
BIRMINGHAM, ALABAMA 35253
(205) 871-0380

Depression:
A Way Out
A Christian Biblical View

Published by The Sheep Shoppe
            P.O. Box 531147
            Birmingham, Alabama 35253

First Printing, 1999
Printed in the United States of America

ISBN 0-9634836-3-3

ACKNOWLEDGEMENT

I am deeply indebted to my wife, Mary Glynn, for her patient counsel and the typing of the manuscript.

Two dear couples, Charles and Peggy McCreight and Charles and Patty Renfroe have encouraged me through the last several years to continue working on the book. They have also provided resources that have enabled the book to be completed and published.

Our mentor, Dr. Henry Brandt, provided the insights into Biblical counseling that got us started over twenty years ago. His wise counsel to stay with the Bible in order to find answers for life, has kept me on track. Early on he said, "Sam if you have a Bible verse you have an answer, if not you have an opinion."

Through much learning and praying, the Lord has been faithful to guide me as I sought for guidance to give to those He has led across my path seeking help with their depression.

My desire is that He would have all the credit and praise should you benefit from the following Biblical principles.

CONTENTS

THE FIRST PSALM

Blessed is the man that walketh not in the counsel of the ungodly, nor standeth in the way of sinners, nor sitteth in the seat of the scornful.

But his delight is in the law of the Lord; and in His law doth he meditate day and night.

And he shall be like a tree planted by the rivers of water, that bringeth forth his fruit in his season; his leaf shall not wither; and whatsoever he doeth shall prosper.

The ungodly are not so: but are like chaff which the wind bloweth away.

Therefore the ungodly shall not stand in the judgement, nor sinners in the congregation of the righteous.

For the Lord knoweth the way of the righteous: but the way of the ungodly shall perish. KJV

INTRODUCTION

Depression is an emotional problem that affects one out of seven Americans to the extent that they seek outside help. One in 20 suffers from major depression, and some 15 percent of them will commit suicide. Seventeen percent of Americans will suffer a major depressive episode during their lives. I believe these statistics would hold true for the Christian community. Of the people with major depression, 50 to 60 percent will have a second episode, 70 percent of those who have two episodes will have a third, and 90 percent of those with three episodes will have a fourth. Major depression costs 44 billion dollars each year in the form of medical treatment, lost productivity and social services. Many are depressed and do not seek professional help. They settle for a life of slipping in and out of depression.

What about the future? In a national TV news broadcast on September 9,1996 the World Health Organization stated, "By the year 2020, a combination of:

  Heart disease
  Depression
  Auto accidents

will cause more deaths than infectious diseases, which has been the leading cause of deaths worldwide."

It is stated in a recent national news broadcast that the number of medications taken for depression had doubled in the last year (1998). A recent health magazine stated, "As medical science discovers new cures and treatments every year, depression remains largely a mystery. Yet despite the increased public consciousness about depression and the Prozac pop-culture, many myths about the disease remain." Depression is now accepted by the caring professionals and most of the public as a disease or illness. I was interested in the reference to our culture being, "A Prozac pop-culture!"

I recently referenced the word depression in my computer. At the end of several pages of information there was a list of organizations and places to get help. None of them were churches or any organizations that offer spiritual help. The above magazine article closed with these remarks, "Prozac and other SSRIs (selective serotonin reuptake inhibitors) control the symptoms of depression. They help clear the patient's head long enough for him or her to function normally and receive talking therapy. Depression is a chronic illness for which there is no permanent cure."

A Future Nobel Prize

There were some interesting remarks in the U.S. News & World Report magazine in the January 24,1983 issue. "We don't know if the mind thinking depressed thoughts causes the biochemical changes, or whether the chemical imbalance in the brain is what causes the depression," says Dr. Keith H. Brodie, chancellor of Duke University and president of the American Psychiatric association. "This is where a Nobel Prize is going to be won." As a student of the Bible for more than 34 years, I have collected many Bible verses that relate to the effect of the mental and emotional state on the body. In my life notebook I have over four pages of these verses under the title, "Psychosomatic Bible verses." I continue to add new verses. My conclusion: these verses provide information that, "thinking depressed thoughts causes the biochemical changes." Not only these biochemical changes, but other negative changes in the body can and will occur. These changes will be referred to in several of the following chapters. Maybe I should submit my collection to the Nobel Prize committee! However I don't think the information would merit an award. Even if it did I would have to turn it over to the Lord because it all originated with Him. As far as I know the secular community has not come to a conclusion.

A recent Forbes magazine article concerning suicide and depression, stated, "Most people who contemplate suicide are suffering from depression. Here, too, enormous pharmacological advances are being made in treating this debilitating condition." Notice again the focus on finding newer and better medications for the treatment of depression.

Headlines in a major newspaper in November of 1997 :

DEPRESSION LINKED TO HEART ATTACKS

"Depressed people are more likely to have a heart attack than smokers or those with high cholesterol, according to one of the largest and longest studies on the link between depression and heart disease.

People with depression run about twice the risk of a heart attack than the general population, researchers said this week at a meeting of the American Heart Association in Orlando.

Smoking and high cholesterol are two of the strongest known risk factors for heart disease. But this is, the first time depression has been directly linked to first heart attacks, said researchers from New York's Albert Einstein College of Medicine."

Though the above article was written recently, back in 1947 a well-known medical director at a hospital in Chicago said, "Fatal heart attacks can be triggered by anger in all degrees, depression and anxiety."

A Unique Approach

This book will take a unique Biblical approach in helping you understand depression. My search through the Bible and listening to hundreds of Christian's stories in the counseling room, will be the foundation of the information.

Do you believe someone experiencing God's love, joy, peace and faith could at the same time be depressed? In theory the answer seems apparent. In my personal experience I have found this theory to be true. Could we conclude that if we are depressed and decide to let God's love, joy, peace and faith reign in our lives, we would not be depressed? Help for the depressed is to bring into their experience the control of the Holy Spirit so that the fruit of the Spirit might be theirs.

When we allow negative sinful reactions to accumulate in our life the Holy Spirit is grieved and or quenched and fellowship with the Lord is broken. In this condition it is impossible to experience the fruit of the Spirit. So the first step is to deal with these sinful reactions according to the Bible and be free of them. Also, we will discover the root cause of these sinful responses. Then there will be a presentation of a series of Bible verses that promise God's control over the root cause. When all of this is brought into experience, you too will realize that it is truly a unique approach! Made possible by our Creator God.

This is not a popular approach and not many agree with it. Therefore it is seldom offered as a solution and so few have the opportunity to benefit from it.

It is interesting to realize that all the information contained in the fields of sociology, psychology and psychiatry have come through research.

This research consists of results gathered through observation and interviews. In contrast, this Biblical approach has come through revelation.

For the past 20 years we have taken this Biblical approach and have had the blessing of seeing many Christians brought out of their depression. The information offered in this book not only showed them how to come out of their depression but also how to prevent going back into depression!

Jesus said, "I have come that they might have life and have it more abundantly." John 10:10b KJV. If His desire is that we have an abundant life, I don't believe it includes being depressed.

God's greatest expression of His love is Jesus dying on the cross for our sins and raising Him up that we might share in that resurrection life.

My prayer and goal in writing this book is to bring to you some insight into the great and boundless provisions that God has for you and in so doing that you might enjoy them.

The major part of the book will provide answers to four questions.
1. What is depression?
2. How do you become depressed?
3. How can you be free of depression?
4. How can you prevent depression?

Other chapters explain the vital role of God's love in relation to depression and the unique benefit of our union with Christ. Also there is a chapter relating these principles to the life of Jonah.

Accomplishing the Goal

John Pulitzer of newspaper fame said, "Put it before men briefly so they will read it, clearly so they will appreciate it, picturesquely so they will remember it and above all accurately so they will be guided by its light." I have tried to follow this philosophy in presenting this information. If you benefit, then my goal will have been accomplished!

CHAPTER ONE

WHAT IS DEPRESSION?

Webster's original dictionary defines depression as: A sinking of the spirits; dejection; a state of sadness; want of courage or animation; as depression of the mind.

One medical dictionary describes depression as the absence of cheerfulness or hope; a lowering or decrease of functional activity. The absence of hope seems to be a common characteristic of depression. Remaining in depression causes hope to get weaker and weaker, resulting in other adverse changes.

Hope deferred makes the heart sick, but when the desire is fulfilled, it is a tree of life. Proverbs 13:12 AMP

For twenty years I have accumulated literature on depression. Each author has given their definition. As the definitions were compiled, it was obvious there was an overlap in the descriptive terms used to describe the characteristics of depression. Listed below are some of the most common characteristics.

1. Hopelessness and despair
   Sad, blue, a feeling of overall gloom, mood fluctuations
2. Apathy
   Losing interest in your usual activities
3. Feeling worthless
   A sense of being useless. Guilt seems to be an ever present factor
4. Changes in physical activities
   Eating, sleeping and sex
   Unusually tired, loss of energy, hard to get up in the morning
5. Loss of appetite or a gain in weight
   Declining interest in food or gorging

6.   Unable to concentrate
     Indecisive, forgetful
7.   Loss of perspective on life
     Family, job
8.   Loss of self-esteem
     Lower sense of personal value, negative attitude
9.   Withdrawal from others
     Fear of rejection, association of over sensitivity with inter
     personal relationships
10. Difficulty in handling emotions
     Especially anger, also resentment and guilt
11. Self pity
     Constantly focusing on self and the circumstances

Depression is diagnosed on the basis of the presence of some, many, or all of the above characteristics or symptoms.

If you have not read the introduction, please go back and read it. It contains information that will help you better understand the rest of the book.

Using a Biblical approach and applying it to many who have come seeking help, I would say that basically depression is the result of the accumulation of negative responses. These responses occur inside of us and may be expressed or repressed or both. The characteristics or symptoms are caused or directly related to these negative responses. Even the secular professionals, for many years, have stated that depression is the result of "anger turned inward." (I am not sure how you can turn something inward that is already inside?)

When a person is becoming depressed, and continues to perpetuate the same thinking and behavior, the depression is reinforced.

Symptom Reduction

A Christian psychiatrist friend recently told me that, "Psychiatry for the nineties has as its goal: Symptom Reduction." We are treating a, "Cluster of symptoms resulting in pain." He also stated that the TV ads for the biological medications are very misleading.

The idea of removal or cure seems to be foreign in the thinking of those who are responsible for the treatment of depression. Using a Christian Biblical approach not only alleviates symptoms but deals with and removes root causes. Using this approach allows the idea of removal and cure to become a reality.

For the Word that God speaks is alive and full of power - making it active, operative, energizing, and effective; it is sharper than any two edged sword, penetrating to the dividing line of the breath of life (soul) and (the immortal) spirit, and of joints and marrow (that is , of the deepest parts of our nature) exposing and sifting and analyzing and judging the very thoughts and purposes of the heart. Hebrews 4:12 AMP

The Bible proclaims itself to be powerful enough to solve any and all problems that His creatures might experience. The question before us is: will I allow God and His Word to work for me in the way that He has promised?

When I first became a Christian my Bible teacher, Elizabeth Newbold, said, "Don't argue over how sharp the sword is, just stick em with it!!" Be prepared and submit to the work of the sword!

CHAPTER TWO

HOW DO YOU BECOME DEPRESSED?

Earlier in defining depression, I stated that depression is an accumulation of negative reactions which build up inside. As we examine these reactions or responses in light of the Bible we will see that they are called sin. There are five of these responses, that if allowed to build one on the other and multiply, will eventually lead to depression. The characteristics or symptoms listed in the previous chapter are a direct or indirect result of the accumulation. The sequence of these responses follows one after the other. I have chosen to call the sequence a Chain Reaction.

The following five chapters will deal with the components of the Chain Reaction. The first one to consider is the natural tendency to want our own way.

CHAPTER THREE

HAVING TO HAVE MY OWN WAY

All we like sheep have gone astray; we have turned every one to his own way; and the Lord has laid on Him the iniquity of us all. Isaiah 53:6 KJV

Many times when things don't go our way, we become disappointed. Below is a list of many events, or circumstances in life that bring on or allow for disappointment.

1. Death of a loved one
2. Marriage partner (or lack of)
3. Divorce
4. Unwanted pregnancy
5. Children (or lack of)
6. Loss of a job
7. Job responsibilities
8. Financial condition
9. Health (or lack there of)
10. In-laws
11. Friends (or lack of)
12. Society
13. Vacation (or lack of)
14. Church

This is one of my favorite verses:

You are a poor specimen if you can't stand the pressure of adversity. Proverbs 24:10 TLB

We all experience times of disappointment. This experience is actually a reaction. We are disappointed when things do not go the way we planned, worked toward or even prayed for.

Disappointment in and of itself is not wrong. The question is how we react when we are disappointed. Are we angry in the face of disappointment or are we comfortable in the face of disappointment? Only our reactions can bless or burn. If we are angry, we are wrong. This anger can cause spiritual, emotional and even physical damage. Anger will be dealt with in the next chapter.

Isaiah 53:6 explains why we experience the feeling of disappointment in a clear and concise way. This verse states: All we like sheep have gone astray; each has turned to his own way; but the LORD has laid on Him the iniquity of us all.

In this verse the LORD is referring to God the Father. The Him is referring to the coming Messiah, the Lord Jesus Christ. Jesus Christ came into time so the Father could lay on Him the iniquity of us all. If this is what the Father planned for His Son, don't you think we should have a clear understanding of - "the iniquity of us all"? The word iniquity is a singular term. It is not plural! Jesus Christ had laid on Him one singular thing common to all. The verse begins and ends with "all". We are all involved! What is this "iniquity of us all"? We have the answer in the first half of the verse: All we like sheep have gone astray each has turned to his own way or each has to have his own way. This is at the very heart of selfishness and is the nature of human nature!!

Selfishness

Webster's original dictionary defines selfishness as: the exclusive regard of a person to his own interest or happiness; that supreme self love or self preference, which leads a person in his actions to direct his purposes to the advancements of his own interest, power, or happiness, without regarding the interest of others. In its worst or unqualified sense, is the very essence of human depravity, and stands in direct opposition to benevolence, which is the essence of divine character. As God is love, so man, in his natural state is selfish.

"When a man is all wrapped up in himself he makes a pretty small package." John Ruskin

Other ways of expressing this might be:
> My expectations were not met.
> She doesn't meet my needs.
> I am tired of being let down.

He just doesn't see it my way.

Our plans didn't work out.

He doesn't pay enough attention to me

When I understood the meaning of the word iniquity, verses in the Bible that contained this word took on new meaning. Many verses began to support the Biblical principle that at the root of all our problems is the desire to have things go our way.

DAVID AND INIQUITY

Psalm 32 presents a clear picture of this fact. The events leading David to write this Psalm are found in II Samuel chapter 11. Verses 1 and 2a, "And it came to pass, after the year was expired, at the time when kings go forth to battle, that David sent Joab, and his servants with him, and all Israel; and they destroyed the children of Ammon, and besieged Rabbah. But David taried still at Jerusalem. And it came to pass in an eventide, that David arose from of his bed."

In the Wrong Place at the Wrong Time

This gives us a clear picture of David's spiritual condition. At a time when kings go forth to battle what was King David doing tarrying in Jerusalem? He was accustomed to leading his troops in battle but now he sent all Israel out to battle while he stayed home. One day in the eventide (late afternoon) David got out of his bed. To me this further discloses his condition. Is this a time for the king to be getting out of bed? Here is clear evidence that David was doing what he wanted to do and not what he knew he should be doing.

II Samuel chapter 11 verse 2b, "David walked upon the roof of the king's house and from the roof he saw a woman washing herself: and the woman was very beautiful to look upon." In verses 3-5 David inquired about the woman, found out she was married to Uriah, sent for her, lay with her and later received word that she was with child — his child!

We need to be reminded of who this man was:

1.   The king of Israel
2.   A man after the heart of God

As king, David had acted also as judge. He was very familiar with the law of God regarding adultery. On occasion David played a part in sentencing people to death for committing adultery. Death by stoning, the most cruel and painful means of execution. David must have heard the agonizing cries and screams of pleas for mercy as many suffered unto death. David was fully aware that the king was not above the law. He was open and confident about what he was doing as he brazenly sent his own messengers to bring this married woman to him. This gives us further insight into David's spiritual condition.

Notice that he sent messengers, at least two or more. This is more evidence of his spiritual/emotional condition. This resulted in poor judgement. The Jewish law required two witness to condemn a man to death for committing adultery.

Later David sent a letter to Uriah's commanding officer instructing him to place Uriah on the front line of the next battle. David wanted Uriah killed. David sent the letter to Joab, the commander, by Uriah! Another evidence of poor judgement.

When Self is in Control

David's strong desire to have his way over ruled:
1. His knowledge of the law of God
2. His commitment to his God
3. His fear of the penalty of the law of God
4. His reputation (remember this is the man of whom it was said — a man after the heart of God)
5. His commitment to his country
6. His conscience
7. His personal concern for Bathsheba and her husband
8. His desire to remain in power
9. The preservation of his spiritual and emotional stability

Enough time had lapsed between these events and his experiences of Psalm 32, for him to suffer spiritually, emotionally and physically.

Blessed is he whose transgression is forgiven, whose sin is covered. Blessed is the man unto whom the Lord imputeth not iniquity, and in whose spirit there is no guile (deceit). Psalm 32:1,2 KJV

In these first two verses David describes the relief one gets, and that he had gotten, when their sin and or transgression has been forgiven and covered. Also a man is blessed when there is no guile or deceit in him.

My initial tendency when I have unconfessed sin in my life is to justify, rationalize and be defensive, or as David says deceitful. I am deceitful to myself and to God.

When I kept silence, my bones waxed old through my roaring all the day long. For day and night thy hand was heavy upon me: my moisture is turned into the draught of summer. Selah.Psalm 32:3,4 KJV

David describes the effects of keeping silent or as the Amplified Bible says, "Before I confessed". To confess means to agree with God. Possibly David's rationalizing and defensive attitude may have sounded like this, "I was in a weakened condition, Lord when I looked on the roof top and saw the beautiful woman bathing." Or, "Lord, you know I am just human." "You do understand, don't you, Lord?"

This doesn't sound like someone who is agreeing with God! David is advising us to drop our deceitful spirit and attitude.

What were the results of not confessing his sin?
1. His bones waxed old.
   His spiritual condition has begun to affect him physically. The Amplified Bible says, "His bones were wasting away." Possibly David was experiencing an aging process that had rapidly increased. As you know the bones are attached to each other through the joints. Currently, several of the top ten prescribed drugs are for disorders related to the joints.
2. A roaring going on inside me all the day long.
   The foot note in the Pilgrim Bible says, "The roaring of David's conscience made him sick and weak because of unconfessed sin." When I have done something I knew was wrong, I have experienced a roaring in my head. Many people with migraine headaches describe this same condition.
3. Day and night thy hand was heavy upon me.
   Again David is referring to his inner awareness of God's displeasure. No Christian should have any difficulty identifying with this.
4. My moisture is turned into the draught of summer.
   The Pilgrim Bible footnote says, "In Judea for a month every year in the late summer there was no rain, and all the land became dry and parched and barren. Such was David's life until he confessed his sin."

I can recall a dryness occurring in my mouth when I have sinned, especially if there was a high risk of being caught. I remember speeding on the highway and looking in the rear view mirror. There was a bright blue revolving light on the car behind me. As the highway patrolman walked to my car there was a dry chalky taste in my mouth. I believe this is what David was trying to communicate to us.

Many depressed people I have counseled with have used similar terms in describing their condition. Therefore, I have safely concluded David was describing his own long standing depressed state.

Selah

The last word in verse 4 is Selah. This means as the Amplified Bible reads, "Pause and calmly think of that." It would be to our advantage to pause and calmly think on what David has just said. The medical profession is now saying that more than 80% of the hospital beds in America are filled with people whose medical problems originated with emotional disorders.

What they call emotional disorders, the Bible calls a sinful condition! More recently these reactions leading to emotional disorders are referred to as, "negative emotional reactions." It is more socially acceptable to be known as one who has negative emotional reactions than to be known as a sinner!

Dr. Henry Brandt says he can remember when a very damaging transition took place in America. Suddenly sin became a disease or an illness and now instead of a spiritual problem we have a psychological problem.

The Key to the Psalm

I acknowledged my sin unto thee, and mine iniquity have I not hid. I said, I will confess my transgressions unto the Lord; and thou forgavest the iniquity of my sin. Selah. Psalm 32:5 KJV

This verse is the heart of the Psalm. It clearly discloses the fact that having to have our way or iniquity is at the root of our problems. David says he acknowledged his sin unto the Lord and he did not hide his iniquity. There is a separation of the terms sin and iniquity. David is now confessing his sin and is not hiding his desire to have his way. He confessed his transgression unto the Lord. David's transgressions were adultery and murder. He had transgressed against the law of God. The verse ends with the key statement, "And thou forgavest the iniquity of my sin." What was David's iniquity? His tendency to do what he wanted to do, even when it was clear that he should not do it.

This sounds like Paul's statements in Roman 7:14-23 and Galatians

5:17. In Roman's 7 Paul said the things he wanted to do, he didn't do and the things he did not want to do, he did. In Galatians Paul said the Spirit wars against the flesh and the flesh wars against the Spirit. He says they are contrary one to the other and that is why he has a problem doing what he knows he should do. My study has shown that the words iniquity and flesh are virtually synonymous.

I trust that what David has declared is now clear to you. There was a cause, iniquity, that led to a result, sin. The word Selah appears again. I hope you will pause and calmly think about this, because if you do, it can be a life changing experience for you as it has been for me.

For this shall everyone that is godly pray unto thee in a time when thou mayest be found: surely in the floods of great waters they shall not come nigh unto him. Psalm 32:6 KJV

David admonishes us to confess our sin when we are first aware of them. If we don't our confidence toward God and the certainty that He can be reached will be weakened.

Thou art my hiding place; thou shalt preserve me from trouble; thou shalt compass me about with songs of deliverance. Selah   Psalm 32;7 KJV

David's confidence toward God is restored. God becomes a hiding place for David. God can now preserve or prevent David from trouble. This reminds me of one of my favorite Bible verses, "This I say then walk in the spirit and you will not fulfill the desires of the flesh."
     Galatians 5:16 KJV

David was aware that he needed a preventive power for the next similar temptation. God compassed David about with songs of deliverance. This verse is summed up in John's first epistle where he states in chapter 3 verse 21, "Beloved, if our heart condemn us not, then have we confidence toward God." Selah appears again at the end of verse 7. Surely this is worth pausing and calmly thinking about!

God Speaks

I will instruct thee and teach thee in the way in which thou shalt go: I will guide thee with mine eye. Psalm 32:8 KJV

Here the person speaking is not David but God. God promises David that he will instruct him and teach him in the way he should go. God will guide him with His own eye. This promise is to anyone who has met the conditions that David met. He wanted to get back into fellowship with his

God and to find some prevention from a recurrence (thou shalt preserve me from trouble) the next time he is in a similar circumstance. His confidence that God would guide him was restored. Those conditions: confess both his iniquity and the resulting sins. He also confessed his transgressions against the law of God.

Do you desire God's instruction, teaching in the way you should go and a confident assurance that God will guide you with his own eye? Your desire can be fulfilled if you will follow David's instructions. All the promises and provisions in verse 8 are related to the work of the Holy Spirit. This is especially true of the New Testament teaching. David not only confessed his iniquity, his transgressions and his sins, which left him clean but empty, but yielded himself afresh to God's control. He could not risk the danger of remaining empty for the tendency is to slip back and be influenced, filled with or controlled by his old iniquitous nature.

These instructions of David are not an isolated set of instructions, but are consistent with others who desired to closely maintain their fellowship with God.

God's Chemotherapy

Suppose you had been watching small lymph nodes gradually increase in size just underneath your skin in the upper part of your body. After a few weeks your concern leads you to a surgeon's office. During his examination he becomes very suspicious and makes X-rays. The X-rays reveal a tumor in your chest. He explains that the cancerous cells from this primary site tumor have spread to the lymph nodes. As the doctor points this out, he consoles you by saying that you should not be too alarmed because he will remove the involved lymph nodes. He continues by saying this is a relatively painless procedure and can be done under local anesthesia in his office. The doctor tells you to expect a continual recurrence of these lymph nodes. You will need to return each month and he will remove the new involved lymph nodes.

What if your surgeon told you this? What would you do? I tell you what I would do! I would find myself a new surgeon! I need a surgeon who would deal not only with the lymph nodes but also the tumor in the chest that is the cause of the involved lymph nodes! To keep our analogy intact, the new surgeon would have to inform you that the mass in the chest is inoperable.

However there is good news. There is a very effective well proven chemo therapy treatment that can control the cancer. This will, he explains, keep the cancer from affecting the rest of the body and you should have fewer and fewer involved lymph nodes. We can't totally prevent their recurrence. He continues "this is not due to the lack of strength of the chemical but upon how diligent and faithful you are in applying the chemical". He concludes with a reminder that this is a very powerful tumor.

Many Christians go through life dealing only with the lymph nodes (sins) and not using God's provision for the primary site (iniquity, the tendency to have to have my way). God's "chemotherapy" became available about two thousand years ago. These Christians are puzzled and discouraged because the lymph nodes continue to recur at the same rate. They have missed out on the vital good news of God's provisions in Galatians 5:16, But I say, walk and live habitually in the (holy) Spirit — responsive to and controlled by the Spirit; then you will certainly not gratify the cravings and desires of the flesh — of human nature without God. Amplified Bible

To paraphrase this in light of our analogy, "but I say, walk and live habitually with God's chemo therapy (the Holy Spirit) applied to your primary site tumor (your cancer of iniquity) and it (He) will control this cancer in such a way that you will have fewer and fewer involved lymph nodes (sins)." Does this appeal to you? Have you tried God's chemo therapy for your cancer — iniquity?

This is at the very heart of God's good news to us, don't delay another day without taking advantage of it!

Listed below are other verses that separate the words iniquity and sin:
1. For I will declare mine iniquity; I will be sorry for my sin. Psalm 38:16 KJV
2. Wash me thoroughly from mine iniquity, and cleanse me from my sin. Psalm 51:2 KJV
3. Hide thy face from my sins, and blot out all my iniquities. Psalm 51:9 KJV
4. Thou hast forgiven the iniquity of thy people, thou hast covered all their sin. Selah. Psalm 85:2 KJV
5. Thou hast set our iniquities before thee, our secret sins in the light of thy countenance. Psalm 90:8 KJV
6. We have sinned with our fathers, we have committed iniquity, we have done wickedly. Psalm 106:6 KJV

There is a verse in the New Testament that strongly parallels Isaiah 53:6.

It is Titus 2:14,15 KJV. Who gave himself for us, that he might redeem us from all iniquity, and purify unto himself a peculiar people, zealous of good works. These things speak, and exhort, and rebuke with all authority. Let no man despise thee.

What are "these things"? All that is in verse 14: gave himself for us, redeemed us from all iniquity, purified unto himself a peculiar people, zealous of good works. These are the things that we need to speak, exhort and rebuke with authority. I have been obedient in doing this through these pages. You need to heed this truth and speak with authority to others about it. Remember Jesus said, "Ye shall know the truth and the truth shall set you free."

The truth in verses 14 and 15 can set many people free. We tend to shy away from confronting people with their iniquity and sin for fear it might offend. We run the risk of them not liking us or even despising us. That is certainly not the concept here. If we don't confront these people they will "despise" us for not telling them the truth!

Anne's Story — Strange Love

A lady came to counsel with my wife, Mary Glynn. She was separated from her husband and wanted to discuss how they could get back together and work out their differences. This lady openly spoke of how angry she was and how she had been playing games with him for 30 years. She had been deceitful in their relationship pretending she liked things he did and said, when all the while, she despised what he was doing and saying.

Mary Glynn told her that it would be impossible to work out their differences as long as she was angry and deceitful. All anger has a measure of revenge in it and to be deceitful is to lie. She needed to rid herself of anger and deceit. The lady did not know how to do that. Mary Glynn asked her what she called anger and deceit. She said she did not know. Mary Glynn enlightened her. She told her that the Bible calls these sins.

This lady said no one had ever called her a sinner. Mary Glynn said it was good news that her problem was sin because that is why Jesus died on the cross. If she would confess her sin, God would forgive her and cleanse her of all unrighteousness.(I John 1:9) Then she needs to ask God to fill her with love and a spirit of honesty. Now she can be loving and honest in dealing with her estranged husband.

She prayed with Mary Glynn and asked God to forgive and cleanse her and to fill her heart with love and an honest spirit. As she left the office she put her arms around Mary Glynn and said, "You are the most loving person I have ever met. God sent you to me this day." Seems strange to call someone a sinner for the first time and have them tell you that you are the most loving person they have ever met!

The truth had set this lady free and she was free indeed. That freedom felt good and she was grateful.

> *There is a power of selfishness -*
> *The proud and willful I -*
> *And ere my Lord can reign in me,*
> *That proud old self must die. Anon.*

Some troubles come from wanting to have our own way; others come from being allowed to have it.

Worldly Contentment

If we think about defining the word contentment, I believe it would be, "having things go my way enough of the time to keep me in my comfort zone." If you are not a Christian you have only this one option. If you are a Christian, you have another option. You can allow the Holy Spirit to control your life and experience the fruit of the Spirit. But all too often we as Christians fall back into living the same way as before and rely on things going our way enough to keep us content. This is always a part of the depressed person's story. There is rarely an expression of this in its basic form but it is strongly implied. Just listen carefully or examine your own life carefully.

Julia's Story — Living Above Your Circumstances

Dear Sam and Mary Glynn,

Just a note to let you know how much I have gleaned from your tape series, "Living Above Your Circumstances." I have been a Christian for fourteen years but didn't know how to deal with the anger in my heart. Because of this, I became depressed. For a period of time I was put on medication. This didn't seem to bring much or any relief. I would blame my periodic bouts of anger on someone else's actions, P.M.S. or my depression.

I suddenly saw that my selfishness (wanting to have my way) created anger and that unconfessed anger brought on depression. I have recognized my sin, confessed and obtained victory over what was destroying my relationships with those I love and stealing my joy.

My son as well as my sister-in-law have understood the same information and have benefited tremendously. My husband and I are so impressed with the material that we have purchased nine sets for friends and family.

May God richly bless you for sharing this information through this tape series. You are actually breaking bread and feeding the multitudes.

Much love,
Julia

I have shared this letter because it is a testimony to the Lord of someone who was freed from their depression by listening to tapes. She dropped her medication and came out of her depression without personal counseling. This story represents someone who was very open to the Lord and His Word.

The series of reactions that leads to depression begins with having to have my own way or disappointment. It is the first term in the chain of reactions. The term with the verse relative to it is shown below.

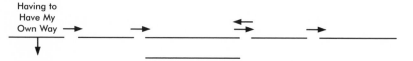

Having to
Have My
Own Way

Isaiah 53:6
All we like sheep have gone
astray; we have turned everyone
to his own way; and the Lord
hath laid on him the iniquity of
us all.

CHAPTER FOUR

ANGER

Let all bitterness, and wrath, and anger, and clamour, and evil speaking, be put away from you, with all malice. Ephesians 4:31 KJV

In the Chain Reaction, the second term leading to depression is anger. In the original Webster's Dictionary printed in 1828, anger is defined as: A violent passion of the mind excited by a real or supposed injury, usually accompanied with a propensity to take vengeance. Varies in degrees of violence. Nor is it unusual to see something of this passion aroused by gross absurdities in others, especially in controversy or discussion. Anger may be inflamed till it rises to rage and a temporary delirium.

Vines Expository Dictionary of New Testament Words defines anger this way, "Suggests a more settled or abiding condition of mind, frequently with a view of taking revenge."

"In the Bible, man is shown as indulging in anger as the result of self-centered disappointment when expectations are thwarted. Anger is portrayed as detrimental to the individual experiencing it and everyone around him. Jesus, in fact, said that a man who is angry with his brother has committed the moral equivalent of murder." (author unknown)

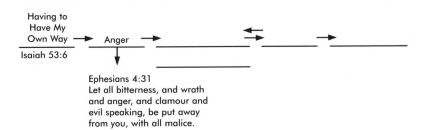

Having to Have My Own Way → Anger →

Isaiah 53:6

Ephesians 4:31
Let all bitterness, and wrath and anger, and clamour and evil speaking, be put away from you, with all malice.

Ephesians 4:26: Be angry but do not sin; do not let the sun go down on your anger.

Here Paul is quoting a verse found in Psalm 4:4. Listed below are three translations of this verse.

1. Stand in awe, and sin not: commune with your own heart upon your bed and be still. Selah. KJV
2. Stand before the Lord in awe, and do not sin against him. Lie quietly upon your bed in silent meditation. TLB
3. Be angry (or stand in awe) and sin not; commune with your heart upon your bed, and be silent (sorry for the things you say in your heart). Selah (pause, and calmly think of that!) AMP

Vines states the word anger as used in Psalm 4:4 means, "Quiver with strong emotions."

Anger is defined in secular literature in terms of energy. This seems strange when you first hear this thought. The more you think about it you realize it is true. Part of Psalm 31:10 says, "My strength faileth because of my iniquity .." KJV

Think about the last time you got angry and had a fit. How did you feel after the fit? Most answer, "Exhausted!" Think about the time you got angry and did not have a fit. How do you feel walking around with that anger festering inside? Most answer, "Drained, tired, exhausted, weary."

Alexander Pope (1688-1744) stated, "To be angry is to revenge the fault of others upon ourselves."

Elizabeth I (1530-1603) said, "Anger makes due men witty but it keeps them poor."

Horace (65-8 B.C.) said, "Anger is a short madness."

We need to consider what these people of old have truthfully said as they looked at and experienced anger.

Anger is very damaging to your physical health and well being. The medical community is far more concerned with the effects of anger on our emotional and physical health than is the church!

In Dr. McMillen's book, None of These Diseases (pages 58 and 59), he quotes the following from a book by Dr. O. Spurgeon English, "There is an emotional center in the brain from which nerve fibers go out to every organ of the body. Because of the intricate nerve connections, it is understandable how any turmoil in the emotional center can send out impulses which can cause anything from a headache to itching in the soles of the feet.

The emotional center produces these widespread changes by means of three principal mechanisms: by changing the amount of blood flowing to an organ; by affecting the secretions of certain glands; and by changing the tension of muscles".

According to the New England Journal of Medicine, "Anger can be hazardous to your health. It increases your body's breathing rate and raises your blood pressure. It even out ranks cholesterol as the number one cause of cardio vascular disease. The arousal of anger is so toxic that the body takes longer to restore it's equilibrium after an episode of anger than any other emotion."

I read the following techniques recommended for handling anger. This article declared that feelings of anger will escalate if they are left unchecked, so it is important to recognize them in their early, preliminary states and take immediate action.

1. Distance yourself from the situation for at least twenty minutes to one half hour.
2. Blow off steam by engaging in physical activities such as exercising, gardening, or deep, controlled breathing.
3. Avoid strong stimulants such as caffeine and depressants such as alcohol.
4. If all else fails, pray or meditate.

Even the secularist recommends bringing God into the picture, but only when all else fails!

A newspaper article of a couple of years ago stated:

Scientists at Harvard have found that a little bit of anger can more than double the risk of a heart attack.

The latest set of studies, in fact, indicates that hostile people have higher levels of the bad form of cholesterol, and that anger and other negative emotions can alter the chemical balance of the brain. Additionally, researchers have found that healthy people who become depressed in old age are twice as likely to suffer heart attack, stroke and death.

Energy Loss

A friend casually told me that he was not able to work more than one half day because of his son's behavior. This father was quick to agree that he was angry with his young teen-age son. Really, what does the behavior of a teen-age boy have to do with the energy level of his father?

The Bible clearly teaches that the father's reaction to the son's behavior is responsible for his energy level.

The question is — what is your reaction when things don't happen as you planned? Disappointment is a result of something going wrong in your life. We have a choice, we can be angry in disappointment or we can be comfortable in disappointment. If we are honest in our self evaluation we will admit that most of the time we get angry.

How you view your reaction of anger is partly determined by your temperament. In referring to temperaments, there are two ways of handling reactions. We can be expressors or we can be repressors and we all do some of both.

If you are an expressor you will not struggle with recognizing your anger as much as a repressor. The following will help you understand the wrong thinking of a repressor. (I should know, I am one!) Most repressors when asked to describe someone who is angry, automatically, like a programmed computer, think of one who visibly displays his anger. This display can be verbally expressed, throwing something, swinging at someone with your fist, a non verbal communication of disapproval, or merely getting red in the face.

The repressor says to himself, "Since I don't do any of these things, I am not angry." I plead with you to evaluate whether or not you are angry by what is going on underneath your skin! This is vitally important because part of the repressor's natural tendency, indeed his goal, is to hide his anger. He strives hard (don't we) to maintain the proper appearance. We need to be reminded that, "Man looketh on the outward appearance but God looks on the heart." Both you and God will know whether or not you are angry. Be careful, your "computer programming" can deceive you. This will allow numerous reactions and/or responses of anger to build up inside.

Don't qualify whether or not you are angry by the amount of anger you experience. By nature we are defensive about our sinful reactions. Our automatic justifier clicks in. This might be expressed by, "Well I was only a little bit angry therefore I am not concerned." Can you imagine a woman saying she is not concerned because she is just a little bit pregnant? We all know what a little bit of pregnancy looks like 8 months later!

If you want to see what a "little bit of anger" looks like in eight months, if not dealt with, then come sit with me in the counseling room and I will show you. Remember Paul's words in Galatians 5:9 "A little leaven leaveneth the whole lump." A little leaven affects the whole batch of dough and causes it to rise when heat is applied!!

Justifying Anger

The most common trap is to justify or rationalize your anger because of the event or circumstance that revealed it. I became angry during a Christian organization staff meeting because another staff member was being criticized and blamed for something of which they were innocent.

Since I had the correct information and the straight facts, why shouldn't I be angry at this unjust blame and criticism? Really now, I have a right to be angry in this situation! Don't you agree? Sounds familiar doesn't it.

I needed to stop and analyze the situation. Several Christians had unjustly blamed and criticized someone. That is their problem and they will have to give an account to God for it. What was my reaction to this? Anger. Now this is an issue for me and I will have to give an account to God for it.

To summarize: when we have a seemingly "just cause" for our anger, we often deceive ourselves and think it is permissible (and not to be called sin). If we have an "unjust cause" for which we respond in anger, it is easier to see this as wrong (sinful) and we turn to God in confession.

Years ago I heard someone say, "That trying to cover your sin is like the new deodorant called "Stereo", it didn't take away the odor but you could not tell where it was coming from."

All Doesn't Mean All To All Christians

What does God say we are to do with anger? "Let all bitterness, and wrath, and anger, and clamor, and evil speaking, be put away from you with all malice." Ephesians 4:31 KJV Here we are admonished to put away all anger. Possibly you believe there are several kinds of anger. I have tried my best to justify and rationalize my anger and to believe that in certain situations there are exceptions. Yet I keep coming back to that word all! In taking a hard look at my anger and the anger that is a part of people's stories in the counseling process, I have never seen any anger that was beneficial.

Many times we want to place a parenthesis after the word all and say, "Except in my situation."   In all the Bible translations, even the paraphrases I have read, I have never found a parenthesis. You will have to decide if *all* means *all*!

Socially Acceptable

One of our problems in trying to identify anger : we have some much nicer sounding terms for it. They are more socially acceptable. Through the years I have built up quite a collection. I want to share some of the better ones with you.

I was burned up!

I have a short fuse!

I blew up!

I was upset!

I just wasn't myself!

I was beside myself!

I lost my head!

He drives me up the wall!

He fried my shorts!

What does it mean to put away anger? When you "put away" your anger God's way, the result is that the anger is not there any more. Obviously there is only one way and that is to confess it. If you confess, God cleanses you. If we confess our sins, He is faithful and just to forgive us our sins, and to cleanse us from all unrighteousness. I John 1:9 KJV. This cleansing results in it not being there any more. Thus satisfying Paul's admonition to put it away.

The non Christian only has two options, to express or repress their anger. Most secular counseling and some Christian counseling seeks to establish a balance between expressing and repressing. If you express too much you need to learn to repress your "negative emotional reactions", especially anger. If you repress too much, you need to learn to express your anger.

There are places that offer programs for repressors to come for therapy. The therapy consists of closing themselves in a room where they are free to break windows, bottles, lamps and to throw bricks and rocks around the room. You are also encouraged to scream. This seeks to give you a better balance. The cost is $5,000 a year! The words express and repress are terms man has brought into being. These words do not appear in the Bible as a means of dealing with "negative emotional reactions".

"Negative emotional reaction" is a term used by those who prefer not to call it what the Bible calls it — sin. It does sound better to be known as one with negative emotions reactions than to be known as a sinner!

Low Batting Average

Another means of dealing with anger was explained to me in the counseling room. Two Christians from two different nearby states were referred to me by their Christian counselors for continued counselling. Each had experienced a long standing problem with anger and "temper tantrum" problems. After listening to their stories, I asked what had been recommended that they do about their problem. Each one gave the same answer. "When I feel my anger building up inside me, I take a large plastic toy baseball bat, find a tree and beat on it until I sense some relief." I asked if this has worked, why are you still in need of counseling? Each had the same response, "This does bring temporary relief but I continue to have the on going problem with anger." Does this seem like strange counsel, especially from a Christian counselor?

A husband concerned about his depressed wife told me, "She gets depressed, terribly depressed. I have tried to bring hobbies into our lives and other things. I even bought her an organ."

A Better Option

For the Christian, there is a third option - confession. "If you confess your sins, He is faithful and just to forgive you and cleanse you from all unrighteousness." I John 1:9 KJV This is the only way I know to be free, rid of, cleansed from anger.

Where in the Bible does it say if you repress, express or establish a balance, you will be free of or cleansed of your anger? Because Christians have the option of confession does not mean they automatically use it. The natural tendency is to justify our anger and then follow our temperament pattern and express or repress it. We must discipline ourselves to follow that which comes supernaturally and confess it.

Another verse that has helped many, "For man's anger does not promote the righteousness God wishes and requires." James 1:20 AMP

We have various ways of justifying our anger. Rather than putting it away, confessing it, we look inside to examine the anger and decide what we will do with it. Typically there are three questions we will ask in our examination. We use one, two or all three:

1. How much anger came out? "Oh, well, that's not much, I won't do anything about it."
2. How far did it come out of my heart? This is a typical question for a repressor. If it wasn't expressed, shown or manifested then I don't need to do anything about it.
3. What kind of anger is it? We are so sophisticated now that we have a variety of kinds of anger.

In Galatians 5:19-21 we are told that anger is a work of the flesh. In other words, our old nature is the source of the reaction or response of anger. Remember the nature of the old nature is to want its way. Therefore, anger is a common reaction when things don't go our way. We need to remember what Jesus said in John 6:63, "That it is the Spirit that quickens and the flesh profits nothing." Later in Romans 7:18 Paul declares; "I know that in me, that is in my flesh, dwelleth no good thing." To quote one of my favorite Bible teachers, "We are constantly bringing the flesh to God and asking Him to Christianize it."

Do you take "nothing" and "no good thing" literally? Yet today, we believe that by placing an adjective (i.e., righteous) in front of the word anger, we suddenly change its source of origin. When we fall into this trap our focus is on the outward circumstance. We look at who or what provoked the anger rather than at our reaction (inside). This is a favorite means of justification. When the focus is outside, I am not responsible. If I am not responsible then I have nothing to confess.

Years ago I put together this "quip" to help communicate the truth about taking personal responsibility.

The circumstances of life,

The events of life,

And the people around me in life,

Do not make me the way I am,

But reveal the way I am.

This quip doesn't support statements like these:
    "It's not my fault, don't you understand what they did to me?"
    "Don't you care about what he said to me?"
    "Every time she says that it makes me angry!"

These statements offer a defense; that I am suffering discomfort because of what someone said or did to me. This type thinking fosters the victim mentality which is so rampant and popular today.

"Your Anger Can Kill You"

"Your Anger Can Kill You", is the title of an article which appeared in the Readers Digest, August 1989. The article was a condensation of a book by Reform Williams, M.D. The title of the book is "The Trusting Heart: Great News About Type A Behaviour."

Dr. Williams states, "The latest research says that to protect your heart, do something about your temper. The bad news is that hostility and anger can be fatal. They not only raise the odds that you will develop coronary heart disease but also the risk of suffering from other life threatening illnesses. Anger causes an outpouring of adrenaline and other stress hormones which result in measurable physical consequences. It is the accumulation effect of these hormones that add to the risk of physical breakdown in various parts of the body.

The good news is that for more than 2000 years, the world's great religions have taught the virtues of a trusting heart. Scientific evidence has shown that those with trusting hearts will live longer, healthier lives."

The book is not a Christian book. It is interesting that the Bible makes many statements that support "the latest scientific findings." Here are a couple of those statements:

A calm and undisturbed mind and heart are the life and health of the body, but envy, jealousy and wrath are rottenness of the bones.
            Proverbs 14:30 AMP

My son forget not my law; but let thine heart keep my commandments, for length of days and long life and peace shall they add to thee.
            Proverbs 3:1 AMP

In Feb. 1990 Parade Magazine pictured a large heart on the cover. Below it was the question, "Is Anger Killing You?" The subtitle below it read, "New evidence about the heart shows that reducing your hostility can prolong your life." The article inside contained more information from Dr. Williams book. "The driven type A personality is characterized by impatience, ambition and a hard work drive. It is not these qualities that cause the damage. It is the anger. It provokes your body to create unhealthy chemicals. For hostile people, anger is poison. It is the anger that gets you. In one study, high levels of hostility found in healthy men at age 25, are up to seven times more likely to get heart disease or die by age 50."

Dr. Leo Madow a well known psychiatrist and author stated, "Depression is probably the most common sign of hidden anger in our society. More people get depressed because of repressed or unrecognized anger than almost any other symptoms. Most of us have trouble with anger because we don't recognize it in ourselves, or we feel we have to deny it and we push it down inside.

Allowing anger to accumulate inside can cause hemorrhoids and upset stomachs. One of the most common causes of headaches is tension and tension is usually a result of repressed or unrecognized anger. It also can contribute to high blood pressure and arthritis. In arthritis our own anger, rage and frustration can make the crippling worse."

"Some patients have said, "You make me sick" as an expression of anger. Often they will vomit because of repressed anger."

Anger Clinics

An article in a local newspaper contained an interview with a family counselor who has started specializing in analyzing and treating anger. He conducts weekly meetings called Anger Clinics. He said that repressed and pent up anger has reached epidemic proportions. He stated that, "People in this country are supposed to be nice at all times. From the time all are born we are taught that the last thing we should ever be is angry and if we are angry, we should never let it show".

"As a result, you have a whole nation of people walking around with 30 years of anger built up inside of them. All of the anger from the third and fourth and fifth and sixth grades is still in there."

"Most people know they don't like being angry but they spend a large percentage of their time being angry anyway. Life makes some people angry every 10 minutes."

Another Answer: Flexibility

An article in a recent USA today newspaper was titled, "Anger extremes take toll — flexible men have lower cholesterol." The following two paragraphs stated that men who either erupt in rage at the drop of a hat or who usually stuff down their anger may be headed for heart attack city, even if they take different routes to get there.

The healthiest cholesterol ratings belong to men who handle anger in a "flexible" way. They are neither meek nor combative — in a new study of 116 middle age pilots."

For vexation (irritated, disturbed in mind) and rage kill the foolish men, jealousy and indignation (righteous anger, dignified wrath) slay the simple. Job 5:2 AMP The footnote in the Amplified Bible regarding this verse, "This was written many centuries ago, but physicians and psychiatrists are continually emphasing the importance today of recognizing the principle it lays down, if one would avoid being among the constantly increasing number of the mentally ill and those killed by avoidable illnesses."

Other Bible verses regarding the damaging effects of anger:
Cease from anger, and forsake wrath; fret not yourself; it tends only to

evil-doing. Psalms 37;8 AMP

Good sense makes a man restrain his anger, and it is his glory to overlook a transgression or an offense. Proverbs 19:11 AMP

Wrath is cruel and anger is an overwhelming flood.Proverbs 27:4a AMP

He who is slow to anger has great understanding, but he who is hasty of spirit exposes and exalts his folly. Proverbs 14:29 AMP

He who is slow to anger is better than the mighty, and he who rules his own spirit than he who takes a city. Proverbs 16:32 AMP

Make no friendships with a man given to anger, and with a wrathful man do not associate, lest you learn his ways and get yourself into a snare. Proverbs 22:24 & 25 AMP

He that is soon angry dealeth foolishly.....Proverbs 14:17a KJV

The north wind brings forth rain; so does a backbiting tongue bring forth an angry countenance. Proverbs 25:23 AMP

This is God's replacement verse for anger and is shown above the word anger in the diagram.

And be ye kind one to another, tenderhearted, forgiving one another, even as God for Christ's sake hath forgiven you.Ephesians 4:32 KJV (see reference below, in the diagram)

As we build the Chain Reaction diagram the second term, along with the appropriate verses, is shown below.

Ephesians 4:32
And be ye kind one to another,
tenderhearted, forgiving one
another, even as God for
Christ's sake hath forgiven you.

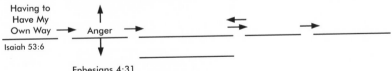

Having to
Have My
Own Way → Anger →

Isaiah 53:6

Ephesians 4:31
Let all bitterness, and wrath
and anger, and clamour and
evil speaking, be put away
from you, with all malice.

CHAPTER FIVE

BITTERNESS OR RESENTMENT

Let all bitterness, and wrath, and anger, and clamor, and evil speaking, be put away from you with all malice. Ephesians 4:31 KJV

Looking diligently lest any man fail of the grace of God; lest any root of bitterness springing up trouble you, and thereby many be defiled; Hebrews 12:15 KJV

And forgive us our debts, as we also have forgiven (left, remitted and let go the debts, and given up resentment against) our debtors. For if you forgive people their trespasses — that is, their reckless and willful sins, leaving them, letting them go and giving up resentment — your heavenly Father will also forgive you. Matthew 6:12 and 14 AMP

The foolishness of man subverts his way (ruins his affairs); then his heart is resentful and frets against the Lord. Proverbs 19:3 AMP

The definition of bitterness: extreme enmity; affliction; deep distress of mind. A root of bitterness producing bitter fruit.

The definition of resentment: a feeling of displeasure and indignation; from a sense of being injured or offended.

Someone has said that resentment is our way of punishing ourself for another persons behavior.

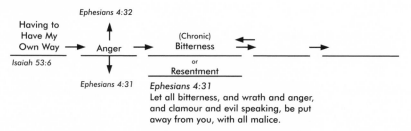

Flames to Glowing Coals

If anger is not dealt with or ignored, I believe it turns into bitterness. An angry response inside of us is typically an "acute" response. In the diagram, the word acute appears above the word anger. At the end of this chapter you will see the word chronic appearing above the word bitterness. In other words, when the acute response of anger is not dealt with it takes its chronic form, bitterness. Lighting a charcoal fire in your grill provides a good illustration. The charcoal is placed in the grill. Next the lighter fluid is squirted on the charcoal. Then a match is thrown into the charcoal. The flames leap from the grill but soon die down and we are left with the long standing glowing coals.

Anger is a sudden response (acute) that leaps up inside of us. But soon it dies down and we are left with the long standing coals of bitterness (chronic anger). In other words much of our bitterness is the chronic form of anger. Bitterness can also be a reaction that is not in the form of chronic anger. However I can not imagine ever being bitter and not having some anger present at the same time.

My Problem is Sin?

Bitterness in the Bible is and should be listed among other reactions the Bible calls sin. In Ephesians 4:31 we read: Let all bitterness, wrath, anger, clamor and evil speaking be put away from you with all malice.

The term put away has meant many things to different people. In my study I found that the result of putting it away, is that it is not there any more. It is removed, gone. So regardless of the instruction given on the efforts made to put it away, the result must be that it is gone. Personally in my studies of the Bible there is only one way to remove bitterness, or any sin and that is to confess it to God. This precludes that you believe your bitterness is sin. Several times in relating this to my counselee they suddenly looked surprised or shocked. Dr. Peeples, are you suggesting that my problem is sin? When I answer in the affirmative most of the time there is an immediate defensive action taken. How could you say that? I told you I am a Christian. I have been a deacon in my church for years, I am a Sunday School teacher and I go to church every Sunday and Wednesday night. The list could go on and on.

Several times I have said, "I am sorry if I have offended you, but first let me go on record as saying I am NOT for sin. Yet I hope that today your problem is sin. For you see Jesus died for your sins and if you confess them to God, He will cleanse you. Personally I don't know of any other way to be free of your anger and bitterness."

The Need of a Road Map

Several years ago the, "Wall Street Journal" placed an advertisement in the "New York Times," reprinting one of its editorials about the moral dilemmas that appear daily on television. The tag line of the piece read: "When was the last time you had a good conversation about sin?" In the article were the following lines:

Sin isn't something that many people, including most churches, have spent much time talking about or worrying about...but we will say for sin — it, at least, offered a frame of reference for personal behavior. When the frame was dismantled, guilt wasn't the only thing that fell away. We also lost the guide wire of personal responsibility...everyone was left on his or her own. It now appears that many wrecked people could have used a road map. Thomas Long, in a recent editorial, commented that this is a "surprising call for someone to step forward and to teach the culture how to confess, once again, its sin."

The Connection

Psychiatrist Sadler writes, "A clear conscience is a great step toward barricading the mind against neuroticism." Psychologist Henry C. Link also sees the connection between sin and disease: "The emphasis on sin has largely disappeared from the teachings of religion...at the very time when psychology has discovered its importance and extended its meaning." None of These Diseases ,S.I. McMillen, page 66.

This quote was in 1952. Nothing has changed since then and in my opinion is more true today than then.

The secular literature I have read does not teach how to be free of "negative emotional reactions" — sin. The best they have to offer is to try and relieve the symptoms both emotional and or physical. The most common means is through drugs. They are effective most of the time in making you feel better. Because we are such emotionally oriented creatures, in order to feel better, we will do whatever it takes. If you have wondered if medication removes the cause then quit and after a few weeks see if the symptoms return.

"Coping Skills"

Another popular means is to teach or equip people with coping skills.

Coping means "learn to live with". Where in the Bible does it recommend that you should learn to live with your sin? If the effort is to help you learn to live with your circumstances and the people around you then I believe that would be helpful. However learning to cope with your circumstances will not do anything for your heart. Neither will it take away any unacknowledged, unconfessed sin.

The trouble from a root of bitterness is often blamed on ones temperament. The same "therapy" that is often offered for anger is offered here. This is the detailed story of one of the counselees mentioned in the previous chapter. All of us either repress or express. We all have some of each but we are more one than the other. The repressors are advised to be more expressive and the expressors are to be more repressive. You know, strike a balance.

The venting of ones anger and or bitterness is often a recommendation.

Another Low Batting Average

I met with a man in his late twenties who had just been transferred to Birmingham. He had been going for counseling during the past several years. First to a secular psychologist then to a Christian counselor. He shared his background with me. "My father never paid any attention to me. He was a bitter, cold and indifferent man. My grandfather was a bitter, hostile selfish man who abused my grandmother. He often spent the night with the woman next door. Today my father is grossly overweight and has many physical problems. He is almost incapacitated. I know my spiritual problem is affecting me physically. I am getting allergies. I react to caffeine and certain medications. I know I am bitter and have tried to deal with it. I want to get married but I am afraid to consider it because I may turn out like my father and grandfather."

I asked what counsel he had received and what he was trying to do to get better. He replied, "I was told to go get a large plastic baseball bat and every time I thought about my father and am bothered by my bitterness, to go and beat on a tree and work it out of me. I really never did think that was Biblical. Yet my counselor told me it was dangerous to keep all this bottled up inside of me. Occasionally I confess my sin but I seem to slip back into it. What would you recommend?"

Apparently he still didn't have any answers that brought lasting change. There was a need to repent (change his mind), and confess his anger toward his father and grandfather. Then ask the Lord to fill his heart with love for his father and grandfather. To give love a chance to protect him. Also he needed the Holy Spirit to be in control of his life and as a part of that to allow the Holy Spirit to control the flesh.(Gal.5:16)

"Defeeted"

A woman came seeking help and told of her bad marriage. There was very little communication with her husband. He complained about her behavior and the way she managed the house. As we talked she admitted she was angry and bitter. I asked her what she tried to do for relief. She quickly said she would go immediately after an argument, put on her walking shoes and go for a 4 mile walk. But now she had injured her foot, it is swollen. She couldn't walk that far. In fact, she said that is why I am here. I am going crazy because I can't take my walks.

For best results —
follow the instructions
of the Maker

Isn't it amazing that we don't turn to the Bible, the Manufacturer's Manual, to seek information. Let me assure you that it does contain the necessary information to make an accurate diagnosis and offers God's, the Manufacturer's, prescriptions.

Pills for Problems of the Heart?

All of these people who have come have one thing in common. They have a heart problem. I don't recall anyone denying this. When drugs (street), alcohol or prescribed drugs (legal) are used for problems of the heart they really aren't effective in basic change. Jesus spoke directly to this when He said to his disciples in Mark 7: 18 and 19 KJV, "So He said to them, "Are you so without understanding also? Do you not perceive that whatever enters a man from outside cannot defile him, because it does not enter his heart, but his stomach, and is eliminated, thus purifying all foods." Although He said this pertaining to foods not causing negative effects, I believe it also applies to anything taken orally or I.V. seeking positive relief and results. Why don't they work? They don't enter the heart!! Remember these are the words of our Creator!! If you have a heart problem, why would you expect something put into your mouth to change your heart?

Certainly I am for certain medications but should we take them for relief of the symptoms of our sins? Or to ask them to act as a substitute for the fruit of the Holy Spirit? If you are a Christian you definitely have a better option.

The Bible speaks further to this in Ephesians 5:18 AMP "And do not get drunk with wine, for that is debauchery: but ever be filled and stimulated with the (Holy) Spirit." Paul is saying you don't need to get your peace, joy or contentment from wine — get it from being filled or controlled by God's Holy Spirit. My intent, God says, is for you to get these things from me.

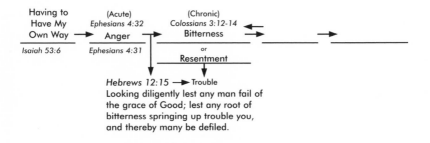

Failing of the Grace of God

In the chain reaction diagram notice that when we get angry, the grace of God is available through confession to cleanse us of our anger. If we fail to avail ourselves of this grace by confessing, then a root of bitterness will spring up in us. If we allow it to spring up, God says there are two results you can count on, one you will be troubled and two, those around you will be affected. (Hebrews 12:15)

The Territory

I will always remember a lady who came for counseling and how her story so accurately related to this verse. Her husband was a traveling salesman and was gone all week. Over a year ago she said he began coming home later and leaving earlier to get back to his "territory". This plus a coldness toward her and virtually no intimacy, resulted in a strong suspension that he was involved with another woman. Finally, she confronted him but he denied it. She was very troubled. The tranquilizer she had been taking for several months did not give her much relief. I asked her how she was reacting to all this. I clarified this by saying what goes on inside of you when the evidence presents itself or you think about it? She readily admitted that at first she was mad but now she was bitter and jealous. This was a very troubled woman. She had not been diligent and had failed of the grace of God to confess her anger. Her root of bitterness had really spread deep into her heart and soul.

I explained to her that her bitterness was the reason for her trouble not her husband's behavior. I assured her that I was not belittling or condoning her husband's behavior. It is obvious she was there, he was not. I needed to help her. We talked about Hebrews 12:15. Also I asked her to read the first part of John 14:1, where Jesus said, "Let not your heart be troubled." Then I asked her, if your heart is troubled, who let it? Because she was so focused on her husband's behavior and her suspicions, she had a hard time seeing that these truths could apply to her. We talked further about confession and replacing her anger, bitterness and jealousy with love. She promised to think about it and made another appointment.

Soon after she left her daughter called to ask about her mother. She has been so worried and was praying for her mother. How did the appointment go? That evening I got a call at home from her son who lived in another state. He shared his concerns and asked about our appointment.

In reflecting on the events of the day, I suddenly realized that this women's story and the subsequent phone calls from her two children had fulfilled prophecy. God says that anyone who fails of His grace and lets a root of bitterness spring up in them, will be troubled. She was troubled! The two phone calls proved that her troubled heart and spirit had affected her two children. I don't know who else was affected but at least her two children were.

The Need To Practice What You Preach

Several years ago we built a house. I was involved during the construction. Many days some of the workmen did not show up as they promised. Two of the sub contractors were very wasteful of materials.

One of the subs tried to overcharge me. I began to fail of the grace of God by not confessing my anger. Soon my anger turned into bitterness. I became troubled and I was constantly thinking about what was happening and justifying my troubled heart. This went on for several weeks before I finally submitted to the truth of Hebrews 12:15 and John 14:1. When I confessed my anger and bitterness and impatience and asked God for His love and peace, my heart was no longer troubled. During those weeks before I confessed, I was conducting a week-end seminar. I was teaching these concepts! I had already started accumulating the material for this book! Parts of those days I left the construction site to go counsel with someone whose heart was troubled!

These truths and principles are easy to forget. My justifying, rationalizing and defensiveness allowed me to see myself as an exception to the truth. I blamed the workmen for my troubled heart. Remember Jesus said, "let not your heart be troubled." If my heart was troubled, who let it? Fortunately after a few days I confessed my sin of anger, and bitterness and I repented. Then I asked God for love for the workmen.

Would you believe we sold that house. We bought another piece of property and started to build another house. It is finished. I did a much better job of remembering not to fail of God's grace. I was quick to confess my sin, trusted the Holy Spirit for His control in my life and moved on!

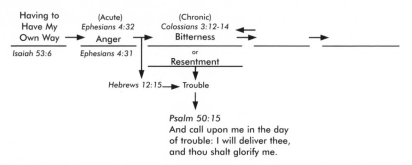

The line going across the page from Heb. 12:15 leads to the next word, Trouble, and the verse, Psalm 50:15. When the root of bitterness is troubling us what should we do? The Bible states very clearly in Psalm 50:15 KJV what to do. "And call upon me in the day of trouble; I will deliver thee and thou shalt glorify me."

I have given a number of examples of what people do in the time of trouble, but here we see that God says we should call upon Him.

If we are this far along in the chain reaction, we have failed to call upon God at least twice. Once at the time when anger came out from the heart.

Secondly when we fail to confess our anger and it takes its chronic form of bitterness.

So what are my options? The first option is the one the Bible recommends, confession. Yet twice that option was not taken. The second option is to seek some means of repressing or controlling the trouble. All too often the second option is taken and leads back up to the next term in the diagram.

The need for relief is growing stronger! What can I do for relief? How do you spell relief? It is not R-O-L-A-I-D-S but G-R-U-D-G-E! This leads us into the next chapter.

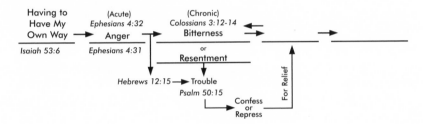

CHAPTER SIX

GRUDGE

Grudge not one against another....James 5:9a KJV

Good sense makes a man restrain his anger, and it is his glory to over look a transgression or an offense. Proverbs 19:11 AMP

Definitions:
A grudge is a secret malice or ill will, as to hold a grudge.

The synonyms are, spite and hatred.

Webster's original dictionary defines it as secret enmity, hatred; sullen malice, ill will; hatred.

In Vines Expository Dictionary it is defined as "Murmur".

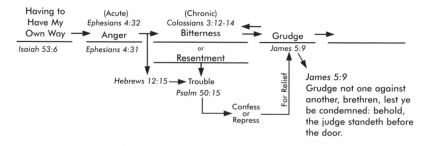

The Hebrew word for grudge is "Nator". It occurs in the Authorized Version translated as, "to keep anger".

A recent article in a local newspaper stated, "Those people who bear grudges should know that the word grudge has evolved from an old term

"GRU", the grunt of a pig!

A national newspaper headline :

<u>BOMBER WITH GRUDGE KILLS FIVE IN FAMILY</u>
"We're trying to find out what method there is to this madness", an FBI agent said.

A Texas newspaper headline:

<u>MASS KILLER DESCRIBED AS LONER WITH GRUDGE</u>

Relief

It may seem strange that a grudge could be used to bring relief from a troubled heart. How does this work?

I have formed a definition of a grudge that will begin to answer the question. A grudge is, "A recalling to the mind of a negative incident from the past". A more practical way of describing these negative incidents is to picture them as "grudge video tapes." Modern technology allows us to record them on video tapes. If we are not careful we can build a large extensive library of grudge video tapes. Typically these are kept in a very secure cabinet in your mind. Why are they guarded so carefully? Because we play them for relief from the trouble which comes from the root of bitterness which was allowed to spring up. In order to get relief, go to the cabinet, turn off the alarm system and remove the padlocks. Look for the appropriate tape. Then insert it in the VCR in your head. As you view and listen to the tape it allows you to justify, rationalize and defend your reactions (anger and bitterness). This is characterized by thoughts such as, "Did you hear what she said?" "Who wouldn't be bitter!" "If she did that to you, you'd be bitter too!" "After all I'm just human!"

When the tape has done its work, remove it from the VCR and very carefully place it back in the cabinet. Why so carefully? You will need it again!!. To continue to play the tapes is harmful because the more we play them, the harder they are to give up. Someone said, "A grudge is like a family heirloom, the older it gets the more precious it becomes!"

Many times I ask people if they believe that grudge bearing is harmful. Their response is always yes. Then I ask them why don't they give it up. This brings a variety of responses, many of which are non verbal. Many seem shocked at the idea, threatened and totally disinterested in giving up their grudge video tapes. When I first started counseling this seemed strange. These people say they have come for help (some in desperate need), agree to the negative effect of the tapes, yet are unwilling to give them up. Later when I understood their use and the role they play in bringing relief, I see why there is great resistance to doing away with them. After all where does one turn for relief if you refuse to open the cabinet? Take my house, my car, my boat, my stocks and bonds but don't mess with my tapes!!

An appropriate quote: the worst fault of all is to believe you have none.

It is important to state here that this relief is temporary. The justifying and rationalizing does nothing for the selfishness, anger and bitterness but it places the blame outside of us and that does bring relief. Because the relief is temporary we will need to return to the cabinet time and time again.

Fertilizing

In our diagram notice that the arrows go back and forth between bitterness and grudge. Each time the video is viewed and heard, new reactions come out of our heart. New anger and bitterness is added to the "pile" inside. The viewing may act as fertilizer to an existing root of bitterness thus causing it to take deeper roots and to spring up higher. Even when I have explained the "fertilizing" effect and it has been understood, there is still an unwillingness to part with the tapes. You see the fertilizer really doesn't work immediately and if I can have some relief now, then I will worry about its negative effects later.

We need to be reminded about the Hebrew word for grudge being translated as "to keep anger". The cabinet represents our anger storage room!

It seems that in the last several years there has been an increase in grudge bearing. And I mean among Christians. Its as if there is an epidemic! Recently an internationally well known leader was asked, "What do you believe is the basic problem we have in the world today?" His answer, "Our cities, states and countries are filled with angry people!" When asked what could be done he was not sure and offered no answer.

Until we are willing to repent and confess our selfishness, anger, bitterness and grudge bearing, there is no real solution. God can cleanse us of these sins and empty out the cabinets.

Love — God's Prevention

God's love prevents us from filling our grudge cabinet. God's love is a part of the fruit of the Spirit. I believe it is by far the major part of that fruit. In I Corinthians 13:4-8a, the 20 characteristics or components of God's love are listed. In our consideration of grudges several of these components play a major role.

First, we see that love does not demand its own way. There is something about love that counteracts my natural tendency to have to have my way. As God's love prevails more and more in my life, my having to have my way is more and more controlled. Let me remind you lest I be misunderstood, that the old (having to have my own way) nature is not irradicated or changed when we become a Christian. It is simply counteracted and neutralized as we allow the Holy Spirit to control our lives. (Gal. 5:16) As this old nature is counteracted, the likelihood of anger and bitterness responding from it is diminished. Without the presence of anger and bitterness there would be no need for relief. No need for relief, no need to play a grudge tape.

Also in the list of characteristics we find, that love does not hold a grudge. So when love prevails there is a direct defense against grudge bearing. Still another characteristic states that love hardly notices when others do it wrong. If we hardly notice when others do us wrong, the chances of recording a grudge tape are greatly diminished.

After we have confessed our sin to God, we need to ask Him to fill us with His love for the individual that provoked our responses. In so doing we will have 3 different means of protection against recording a grudge tape:

1. Does not demand its own way
2. Hardly notices when others do it wrong
3. Does not hold a grudge

There is more about the benefits of God's love in a later chapter.

The Moorage Charge

Grudge bearing is known to cause many different negative physical changes in our bodies. Someone defined an ulcer as, "The moorage charge for a harbored grudge." After a conference, a physician asked me to repeat the definition. He said it was better than the one in his medical dictionary. Since a grudge represents stored anger we can refer back to the list of physical changes in the chapter on anger.

Much time is spent in the counseling room listening to people's stories. Many of these stories are related by means of playing their grudge tapes. Although only the audio portion is coming through, the video is graphically pictured by the drama and emotion used to form the scenes and circumstances.

Nursing a Grudge

I recall a registered nurse coming in for counseling. As she recalled the stories related to her husband's affair (adulterous behavior!), there was much accuracy and detail in the picture she painted. I suddenly realized she was truly, "nursing her grudges."

Some of her accounts were several years old. How do you think she could offer them with such detail and accuracy? The answer is obvious. She played her tapes through the VCR in her mind with great frequency! One of her chief complaints was problems with depression. I asked her if she was aware that she was bearing grudges. Her response was, "yes".We read James 5:9 which states, "brethren grudge not one against another". In other words don't hold a grudge! But the verse and my reasoning and logic were futile in motivating her to give them up. She came in 5 times over a 3 month period. On each occasion she continued to play her tapes. Most of them were new but often she would switch to an old one. Playing these tapes was an effort to bring me up to date and establish the blame for her misery and depression on her husband. She continued to harbor this wrong thinking. At each visit we reviewed what Jesus said in Mark 7. He stated clearly four times that it is not what happens to a person that bothers them but their responses, i.e. what comes out of the heart. She had several years build up of her reactions and wasn't willing to ask the Lord to cleanse her and give her love for her husband. Her own choice robbed her of benefiting from the protection that God's love offered her. She even agreed with me that she was the one suffering from her choice yet she was still unwilling to change.

Several years later she called to make an appointment for her niece. At first she didn't identify herself. When I realized who she was, I questioned her about her situation. Are you still married? "Yes", she said. How are you doing? Her answer, "Much better." Is your husband still seeing the other woman? "No", was her reply. How is your marriage? "Somewhat better". She said she really did not practice what I recommended for several months. Yet she kept thinking about the verses we had read and the Biblical principles we talked about. Finally she turned to the Lord.

The fact that she referred her niece to me displayed some merit to what was shared in our sessions.

Grudge Tape Comments

The following comments were made by people we have counseled with over the past 20 years. Each mentioned depression as a part of their problem. Most of them were seeking help because of their depression. Each statement clearly shows the relationship between grudge bearing and depression.

"She recalls my past sins." Made by a husband whose wife found a strange bobby pin in his car.

"People have made critical remarks about me. I remember them and dwell on them. This has done much damage."

"...been rolling it over in my mind."

" My mind is filled with all this."

" When these things come to my mind, I get hurt again and my depression returns."

" My mind is constantly on my problem, leads to my depression."

" I became depressed after 3 months of marriage — wanted to change my husband. He kept doing things to make me angry — now they keep coming back to my mind. I always wanted to find a guy to replace the one I broke up with, but none could measure up."

"I had a bad childhood and it left an imprint on my mind." (After going over the chain reaction diagram, he said, "This has been the story of my whole life.")

What does the Bible have to say about grudges?

Be gentle and ready to forgive; never hold grudges. Remember, the Lord forgave you, so you must forgive others. Colossians 3:13 TLB

So be done with every trace of wickedness (depravity, malignity) and all deceit and insincerity (pretense, hypocrisy) and grudges (envy, jealousy) and slander and evil speaking of every kind. I Peter 2:1 AMP

You shall not take revenge or bear any grudge against the sons of your people, but you shall love your neighbor as yourself. I am the Lord. Leviticus 19:18 AMP (Notice the command to love after the admonition not to bear a grudge.)

The Lord is merciful and gracious, slow to anger and plenteous in mercy having kindness. He will not always chide or be contending, neither will He keep His anger for ever or hold a grudge. Psalm 103:8,9 AMP

Aren't we glad that the Lord does not hold a grudge!! Since God is love, I guess it would be impossible for Him to hold a grudge.

The memory of the (uncompromisingly) righteous is a blessing, but the name of the wicked shall rot. Proverbs 10:7 AMP

Are your memories a blessing? They are for those who are uncompromising righteous. Righteous means I am in right standing with God and practicing that which I know to be right. Memories recorded on grudge tapes are not a blessing!

Let your eyes look right on (with fixed purpose), and let your gaze be straight before you. Proverbs 4:25 AMP

A grudge always refers to looking back. Look is the first step and gazing is next. It takes the power of God and discipline to maintain a forward gaze. One of my favorite words appears twice in this last verse. The word is let. If your look and gaze are not straight before you, who let them look back? That little word "wreaks" with personal responsibility! It is a good news word because if I let something happen, I can "unlet it"! No one or no circumstance can get between me and the Lord unless I let them! I don't have to let anything come between me and my Lord.

The Best Verses Have Been Saved for Last!

I do not consider, brethren, that I have captured and made it my own (yet); but one thing I do — it is my one aspiration; forgetting what lies behind and straining forward to what lies ahead. I press on toward the goal to win the (supreme and heavenly) prize to which God in Christ Jesus is calling us upward. Philippians 3:13,14 AMP

Doesn't sound like the apostle Paul was bearing any grudges! Notice he doesn't say these 10 things I do or these 5 things I do — but this one thing I do. In no other place in Paul's letters does he refer to this one thing I do. Must be important! And what was that one thing? Forgetting what lies behind and straining forward to what lies ahead. Paul is talking about doing this in order to win a heavenly prize. It seems that heavenly rewards are dependent on forgetting what lies behind, straining forward and pressing ahead. If anyone ever had opportunities to record some grudge tapes, it was Paul. With all his trials, hardships and unjust persecution, he had ample occasion in which to record some tapes and fill his cabinet. It is possible that he did record some "footage" and on occasion he played them. Then having realized the negative effect it was having he chose to rid himself of them. This would help explain his strong admonition to not look back but to look ahead. Grudge bearing can rob you of the abundant life that Jesus offered here and now and your heavenly rewards!

"You can't keep the bird from flying over your head but you can keep it from building a nest in your hair".

Our memories will always be with us. We chose whether or not we will dwell on them. If a negative bird flies over, then shake it out if it tries to nest. If it is a positive bird then it is often beneficial to dwell on it. The Bible actually admonishes us to remember, recall and think about those things which the Lord has done in and through our lives.

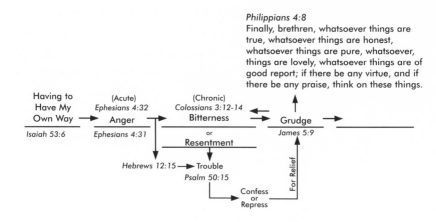

Philippians 4:8
Finally, brethren, whatsoever things are true, whatsoever things are honest, whatsoever things are pure, whatsoever, things are lovely, whatsoever things are of good report; if there be any virtue, and if there be any praise, think on these things.

In the diagram, the reference above the word grudge is Philippians 4:8 For the rest, brethren, whatever is true, whatever is worthy of reverence and is honorable and seemly, whatever is just, whatever is pure, whatever is lovely and lovable, whatever is kind and winsome and gracious, if there is any virtue and excellence, if there is anything worthy of praise, think on and weigh and take account of these things — fix your minds on them. AMP

The Screen

Years ago as I read this list a picture formed in my mind. These words should act as a screen to our minds for what we "think on." I imagined taking a small metal wire screen and cutting it to the size of the entrance to my mental VCR. Then I engraved on each of the wires a qualifying word in the list. I placed it in the VCR. As I inserted a video tape, the contents will have to be screened by the words.

How many of the words that Paul gives to us could be used to describe our grudge tapes? The answer is obvious. The Bible gives us these words as a screen for all our thought life but they certainly apply to grudges.

Only those thoughts which pass through the screen should we think on or fix our minds on. If we insert a tape and it won't pass through the screen then we need to discipline ourselves and quickly remove the tape.

Can you imagine what our thought life would be like if we only thought of those things which are true, worthy of reverence, honorable, just, pure, lovely, kind, virtuous and worthy of praise?

A MEMORY + BITTERNESS = A GRUDGE

Dr.S.I.McMillen in his book, None of These Diseases, stated, "In lifes' frog ponds, perhaps we are able to out-croak our fellows, but it might truthfully be written on many thousands of death certificates that the victims died of "grudgitis." page 69

The Grudgewedge

The wife of an office manager for a large company called for an appointment. She had gone into depression two years ago after she discovered her husband was having an affair. He had broken off the relationship, genuinely repented and sought her forgiveness. She did forgive him but had not really trusted him since then. She was not depressed anymore but was disappointed in her inability to not trust him. I asked her if she ever thought about what had happened? She said very often and at times became preoccupied with the memory.

One of her husbands responsibilities was to keep a large number of secretaries and computer data input people at every station each day. Most of them were women. When emergencies or sickness occurred they called at home. When she answered the phone or realized a woman was on the phone, she listened in on the phone in the bedroom. Her husband had asked her not to do this. She always wondered if this could be another woman he was involved with.

I asked her if she could agree that her constant thinking about the affair was a grudge. She said, " yes." I asked her if she ever reminded her husband about the affair when she was mad about something or was trying to get her way? Again, she said, "yes." Tears filled her eyes. Every time she did this, she felt bad about it and wanted desperately to stop.

She was using the old grudge as a wedge to get him to back down in an argument or to change his mind over a disagreement. She had developed a great tool for getting her way, a "Grudgewedge".

Could I help her she asked. We reviewed the chain reaction diagram and I told her she needed to repent and confess her anger, bitterness, grudge bearing and suspicious attitude to God. Then to ask the Lord to cause her love to increase and abound toward her husband. She was doubtful that this simple approach could help her long standing problem and in her mind a serious complicated problem. Even with the doubt she agreed to give it a try. I reminded her that her selfishness would have to be controlled by the Holy Spirit. If she did not start there then there is little possibility of giving up her "Grudgewedge" since it is her best tool for getting her way.

She returned in a couple of weeks and was amazed at what the Lord had done in her life in such a brief period of time. Even her husband had noticed the change and was very appreciative.

The account below fits very well into the story just concluded.
A man, describing his wife to a friend said, "When my wife gets mad at me she becomes historical." His friend said don't you mean hysterical? He replied, "No I mean historical!"

ANOTHER APPROACH

A director at the National Institute of Health states that between 8-10 million American adults suffer from major depression. Of these she said, perhaps a million or more may not be helped by conventional treatments and could be candidates for more drastic treatments, including electric shock therapy. One of the effects, often labeled a side effect, is persistent memory deficits or loss. I have often thought that this is an attempt to erase a persons "grudge tapes". Since it is often effective in relieving the symptoms of depression this could possibly be the way it acts.

I counseled a woman who was suffering from depression. As she related her story, she stated that she had been given four shock therapy treatments in the previous 6,7 months. Apparently, they had not helped because she was still depressed. Her husband had been having an adulterous relationship for several years. He was now in the process of getting a divorce. She related to me that her mind was filled with what he was doing. These thoughts consumed her mind. She was constantly fertilizing her root of bitterness! It did not take long to restock her grudge video cabinet.

A Shakespearian Portrayal

In Shakespeare's Macbeth, we read:

"Canst thou not minister to a mind diseased,
Pluck from the memory a rooted sorrow,
Raze out the written troubles of the brain,
And with sweet oblivious antidote
Cleanse the stuffed bosom of the perilous stuff which weighs
against the heart.
Give sorrow words; the grief that does not speak whispers the o'er
fraught heart and bids it break."

Shakespeare obviously had a clear understanding of the relationship between what we tolerate in the mind and the way it affects the body.

Our past should be treated as a springboard, not as a hammock!

When we finish the "grudge video tape",having seen and heard what was said and done to us, we begin to feel sorry for ourselves.
Self pity starts to set in.
This leads us to the next term in our diagram.

CHAPTER SEVEN

SELF PITY

For my life is spent with sorrow, and my years with sighing, my strength has failed because of my iniquity; even my bones have wasted away. Psalms 31:10 AMP

Pity - "The feeling or suffering of one person, excited by the distress of another; sympathy with the grief or misery of another."   Webster's original dictionary

When self is placed in front of the word pity, then all of the suffering, distress and misery is directed toward self!

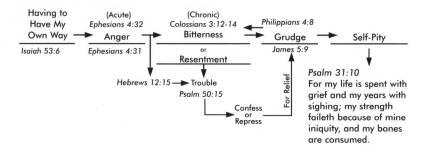

Frank's Story — A Sad Story

Rick called concerned about his brother. Frank had been depressed for several months. He had been to several counselors and was under the care of a psychiatrist. Frank came for his appointment. I was amazed how lethargic he was from his medications. His speech was very slow and slurred. Frank had dropped out of college after his sophomore year due to his depression. His problems at school revolved around two students who teased him and a professor who treated him unfairly in class and in grading his exams. He lived with an aunt who expected him to spend too much time with her. She also required that he drive her to the store and to her other appointments. At the end of his extended story, I asked him how he had responded to the students, his professor and his aunt. He freely admitted he was angry and filled with resentment.

I asked Frank if he was aware that his anger and resentment had led to his depression. His answer was no.

Frank had a clear testimony of when he had become a Christian. When I asked him to consider his reactions as sin and to confess them to the Lord, he began a rather long explanation of justification and defense of his reactions.

I read Eph.4:31. The apostle Paul tells us to put away all anger and bitterness. Frank was aware of this verse but was not interested in putting away his anger or his resentment. He typically began to repeat his story and embellish it.

Finally, Frank was convinced that the unconfessed sin was responsible for his depression. He was not willing to deal with it. Then he said something that is common, "You just don't understand."

I had several more appointments with Frank. Each time we came to the same conclusion: his anger, deep seated bitterness and self pity were causing his depression. Yet he still would not confess his sin and repent.

Two of his family members called out of concern to see if I thought we had made any progress. I reported to them that I didn't see any evidence in Frank of a willingness to change.

Frank did not seek any further appointments. I saw him one year later, walking down a sidewalk. It was a sight I will never forget. Frank was slowly shuffling down the sidewalk with his head bowed over his chest and his hands in his pockets. It appeared that Frank was the same or worse. He represented a walking picture of someone depressed and filled with self pity.

This was a warning for me. I could get into the same condition as Frank if I took the same steps in allowing my sinful reactions to build up inside me.

Depressed Missionary

During a conference trip to Asia, a lady who had been serving with her mission board for the past 11 years, asked if she could counsel with me. During her conversation she said, "I am dependent on others to keep me happy. I want them to encourage me but they don't. Work isn't very challenging, so I spend time thinking about myself. I have some bad times of real depression." Some key parts to her story: Things were not going her way and she spent time thinking about herself — self pity. All of this led to and was a part of her depression.

A Wonderful Testimony From Down Under

Some dear Australian friends, who have for years been teaching this material at conferences, sent us this exciting story of the Lord's faithfulness to His Word.

"The Lord has finally revealed to me the cause of the depression that has plagued me for the past 6 or 7 years. At this stage I am not able to explain in so many words exactly what the cause is and how to deal with it, but I have a solid grip of it in my mind. It has something to do with unconfessed sin, most of which is suppressed anger. This understanding has come through listening to the lectures and reading the material. The joy I have experienced tonight is so wonderful. I feel a tremendous burden lifted from my shoulders. In fact the burden of the "world" in exchange for Christ's. "....for my yoke is easy and my burden is light." I am so thankful to God for showing me the cause of my depression and, the steps necessary to overcome it.

Over the past few years I have wondered if this depression has been my "thorn in the flesh" from the Lord, so that He could keep me following the things of the world. Tonight I feel as though I have sprouted wings and could almost fly!

I am aware that the Lord Jesus Christ has saved me from spiritual death through His blood sacrifice for my sin. Tonight I acknowledge He has also saved me from physical destruction because I believe the depression I had, would, sooner or later, have destroyed me through a nervous breakdown , heart attack, ulcers or suicide.

So now I belong to Christ both physically and spiritually. "A wonderful Savior is Jesus My Lord." I am smothered by the joy of being "free" to belong to Him. May He be glorified through my life!!"
Quite a story!
The Lord is faithful to His promises the world over!

Man at the Pool of Bethesda: Perpetuating Failure

A certain man was there who had suffered with a deep seated and lingering disorder for 38 days.

When Jesus noticed him lying there helpless, knowing that he had already been a long time in that condition, He said to him, "Do you want to become well?" (Are you really in earnest about getting well?)

Matthew 5:2-6 AMP

This is a valid question. Many who continue in depression and self pity don't want to get well! Many years ago I talked to a young 25 year old woman who came for help. She said, "I am often depressed and lonely. I am more unhappy than happy. I am wallowing in self pity. Maybe I enjoy being there."

You can develop a comfortable life style with no responsibility, while people feel sorry for you. Therefore you can do whatever you want because you are depressed!

Verse 7 tells us who he had depended on, "Sir, I have nobody when the water is moving to put me into the pool; but while I am trying to come myself, somebody else steps down ahead of me." He had depended on others and himself and there was no healing!

You would think he would stop repeating what had not worked for 38 years. You need to ask yourself;

1. What are you trying to do to get better?
2. Is it working?
3. How much longer will I keep trying what is not working?

In verse 8, Jesus said, "Get up!"

In verse 9, instantly the man became well and recovered his strength. He took up his bed and walked. Things can happen fast when Jesus is involved!

This man finally turned to Jesus and this is what happened! In verse 14, He said to him, "See, you are well! Stop sinning or something worse may happen to you." Though no specific sin is mentioned in this story, there is obviously a correlation between sin and his condition. Also notice the strong warning against allowing the accumulation of sins because his condition will become worse.

Whatever you have been trying to do to get out of your depression, and you are continuing to repeat the same things, don't you think it is time to try something else? Don't be like this man and continue to perpetuate failure!

A Man Who Forgot to Remember

In I Kings 18, the Lord gave Elijah a great victory over the prophets of Baal. Then Jezebel, upon hearing that the prophets had been slain, threatened to kill him. Filled with fear he fled into the wilderness. In verse 19:4 "he requested that he might die, and said, It is enough; now O Lord, take away my life." An angel of the Lord came to him and said, "Arise and eat." Elijah did so and went 40 days and nights to Horeb. There he hid in a cave. The Lord came and said unto him, "What doest thou here, Elijah?" Then in 19:10 he answers the Lord with his pity party speech, "I have been very jealous for the Lord God of hosts; for the children of Israel have forsaken thy covenant, thrown down thine altars and slain thy prophets with the sword; and I even I only, am left and they seek my life, to take it away." Then Elijah stood in the entrance of the cave. Again the question came, "What doest thou here Elijah?" And in verse 14 he repeats his pitiful story.

Elijah was depressed. He had proceeded down the chain reaction into self-pity. When a person pities himself, he typically goes around boring others with his troubled stories as he plays his grudge tapes. Here Elijah plays his tape for the Lord! Because others are bored with our tapes they seek to avoid us and we are left more and more alone. Loneliness sets in. Soon we are left "talking to ourselves." Each time the tapes are played, new responses come out of our heart and we begin to make cycles through the chain reaction.

My mentor, Dr. Henry Brandt has told me, "If you are a person who has to have your way, then people will get out of your way and you are preparing yourself for a life of loneliness."

SIGHING

In reviewing Psalm 31:10 KJV, "For my life is spent with sorrow, and my years with sighing, my strength has failed because of my iniquity; even my bones have wasted away". We find that the verse has four parts to it.

1. Life is spent in sorrow or self pity
2. My years with sighing
3. Loss of strength because of iniquity (wanting to have my way and the reactions — primarily anger — when I don't get it) Remember that anger is now being defined as energy.
4. Bones are wasting away (beginning to have negative physical changes in the body)

Other appropriate verses:

I am faint and sorely bruised — deadly cold and quite worn out; I groan by reason of the disquiet and moaning of my heart.
Lord all my desire is before You, and my sighing is not hid from You.
My heart throbs, my strength fails me; as for the light of my eyes, it also is gone from me. Psalms 38:8 - 10 AMP

Why are you cast down, O my inner self? And why should you moan over me and be disquieted within me? Hope in God and wait expectantly for Him; for I shall yet praise Him Who is the help of my countenance, and my God. Psalms 42:11 AMP

She looks well to how things go in her household, and the bread of idleness (gossip, discontent and self pity) she will not eat.
        Proverbs 31:27 AMP

All her people groan and sigh, seeking for bread; they have given their desirable and precious things for food to revive their strength and bring back life. See, O Lord, and consider how wretched and lightly esteemed, how vile and abominable I have become!
    Let all their wickedness come before You; and deal with them as You have dealt with me because of all my transgressions; for my sighs and groans are many and my heart is faint. Lamentations 1:11 and 22 AMP

Why does a living man sigh (one who is still in this life's school of discipline)? And why does he complain, a man for the punishment of his sins?   Lamentations 3:39 AMP

But he himself went a day's journey into the wilderness, and came and sat down under a lon broom or juniper tree, and asked that he might die. He said, It is enough: now, O Lord, take my life; for I am no better than my fathers. I Kings 19:4 AMP

Years ago as I listened to peoples stories about their depression, I began to observe something very common while they were speaking. There were frequent interruptions in their conversation as they sighed. I began to expect it in the stories of those who were troubled with depression. So far I can't remember an exception! With some of the stories the sighing was so frequent that I began to count them and note the number on the chart.

World Class Sigher

Marie's story and experience is a vivid illustration and very appropriate.

She is a very successful business woman. For more than thirty minutes, she gave all her reasons for being depressed. To sum up her story, she was depressed because of her situation and circumstances. Her entire story wreaked with self pity. Very typically her story did not include any reactions or responses to circumstances.

As I watched and listened to her, even at the beginning, I noticed she was sighing. "I just could not — sigh — believe my boss said that to me." My husband has become — sigh — more indifferent toward me". "Oh, Dr. Peeples, I hope — sigh — you can help me."

Her sighing was so frequent that I began to count them and note them on her chart. In clocking her for twenty one minutes, she sighed twenty three times! I had clocked others before and after Marie, but she holds the record! She was a "world class sigher."

At the end of her story I led her through the Chain Reaction diagram, relating each step to a part of her story. As I progressed through the diagram, I could see that she was not paying attention and was becoming annoyed. When I finished, I asked for her response. She tried to be nice but finally said that this approach was too simple for her depression. She thought I did not understand the severity of her situation. As she was leaving I asked her to please listen to my tape series on depression. She reluctantly took them. I asked her about another appointment but she said she would call me.

Ten days later she called. I was surprised to hear her voice. She wanted another appointment. When she came into my office she appeared to be relaxed and had a happy look on her face. What a contrast from ten days before! She laughed as she told me how mad she was at me when she left my office. After two days she had a curious desire to listen to the tapes. Finally, she started with the first tape. As she got caught up in them, she became more and more interested and finished the series. The Lord convicted her of the truth of the words and verses in the Chain Reaction. She responded positively and confessed her sin and repented of her actions and reactions. Then she yielded her life afresh to the Holy Spirit's control.

As she sat across from me, I began to watch carefully in order to count the sighs. Toward the end of her appointment, she said she was annoyed at me for looking at my watch so frequently during the first appointment. I confessed that she had caught me counting her sighs. Marie was surprised because she was not aware that she was sighing. When I told her of the count twenty three times in twenty one minutes, she was amazed and laughed that I was counting. I told her the good news. In her fifty minutes that we were together she had not sighed! I questioned her about her depression. Her response, "I have not been aware of the depression since I confessed, repented and yielded." "I have had a couple of short "down times" but they only lasted a few minutes. I couldn't detect any self pity as we talked!

What a testimony! In less than ten days this is what the Lord did for Marie! The Lord is not a respecter of persons so what He did for Marie, He can do for you.

I talked to Marie on the telephone two weeks later. She was doing well. We agreed there was no need for another appointment. I asked her to call me if we needed to get together. She had listened to and reviewed the tapes several times and promised to review them periodically. The next week, Marie sent me a nice card thanking me again for our time together and for telling her the truth.

Some people would resist this story because of how quickly Marie recovered. Since she did have a rapid recovery, she must not have truly been depressed. Or her depression must have been very mild. Let me ask you to resist this thinking and trust the Lord to do for you what He did for Marie!!

Pity Party Etiquette

When self pity sets in we find that we prefer the company of "like minded people". In order to have fellowship with these people, we get together and have a — yes you guessed it — Pity Party!

Were you aware that there is a proper etiquette involved in having a pity party? Let me share the proper procedures for you to avoid any embarrassment. Be sure and check your appearance. If you want pity, how should you look? Pitiful!

at the home of:
- Joe Doe
- 2044 6th Ct. So.
- Pityville, Ala. 35200

time:
2 pm Wed., Feb. 3rd

Be sure and bring 2 of your best Grudge tapes!

As with any party you will need an invitation. On the front should read, "You are invited to a pity party." Then on the inside be sure and include:

Your name

Your address

The date and time

At the bottom of the page be sure to remind them to bring two of their "best" video grudge tapes.

These tapes will be used for entertainment. For at every pity party you will play a game called "Can You Top This". This is done by swapping the grudge tapes around the room. As each video is played, in the VCR in the head, there is a certainty in each participant's thinking that their tape is by far the, "best!" As you watch a tape, the typical comment will be, "That is really a tough situation and I am sorry for you, but you haven't seen anything yet until you see mine!" That is why the game is called, "Can You Top This".

Griping is the best word to characterize the conversation at a pity party. A sign I saw recently would be helpful here. It said, "Lord put your arm on my shoulder and your hand over my mouth."

As you leave the party, whether solo or with like minded friends, after having viewed so many tapes, there is a constant ringing in the mind of "poor me". You will feel more sorry for yourself than before the party.

Cycles

Once we reach self pity in the Chain Reaction, we are candidates for going back through the Chain again. The next diagram shows a long arrow pointing from self pity back to having to have my own way. Once you are back at the beginning, you have completed a cycle through the Chain Reaction.

Several people in calling for an appointment have said they were suffering from, "cycles of depression". One cycle does not result in depression. Neither do three or four. Yet each of us has a tolerance of the number of cycles before we become depressed. As this tolerance is approached, there is an initial awareness of some of the symptoms of depression. When the tolerance is exceeded the symptoms become worse. These cycles can become quite vicious and as they build one on the other the effects begin to compound.

When we are feeling sorry for ourselves or are experiencing self pity, we become sensitive (or touchy). This leads to the next part of the Chain Reaction diagram.

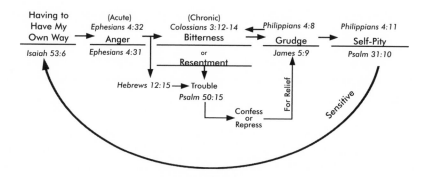

SENSITIVE

Definition: Having keen power to feel; quickly and acutely alive to impressions from external objects or influences. Easily affected or changed by certain outside agents. Very keenly susceptible to stimuli; hurt; easily offended, disturbed, shocked, or irritated by the actions of others; highstrung, tense and touchy.

It is interesting that the dictionary listed a plant called, " The Sensitive Plant." It is described as follows: a plant of the genus Mimosa, so called from the sensibility of its leaves and footstalks which shrink, contract and fall on being slightly touched.

Have there been times when you could identify with this plant?

Many are sensitive in the counseling room and are therefore touchy and very defensive about what I have to say. I know whenever I am sensitive, things just have to go my way more than if I were not sensitive. Because of this it takes less to irritate me or to, "set me off",so I am angry again. If I fail of the grace of God (Hebrews 12:15) and I do not confess my anger and any other sins from the previous cycle through the chain of reactions, then I will move through another cycle. Unless I interrupt this at some point there is a build up inside that moves me toward depression.

The old saying, "the straw that broke the camel's back" provides a good illustration. Initially we may not "feel" the first few straws (sins), but at some point when you approach your limit, you become uncomfortable. Several days or even weeks may go by before you become uncomfortable. Then when you examine your condition, there is a tendency to focus only on the last couple of straws (sins). This is easy to do since they are the most recent. Then they are blamed for your discomfort. The obvious question arises, how could these two or three straws, which may seem insignificant, cause my discomfort? There is a tendency at this point to become preoccupied or even obsessed with these last few incidents or straws. As a counselor I have to remember that the discomfort is not from only the last few straws. Yet most of the time no other information is volunteered. If I try to reach into the bundle of straws beneath the last two or three, typically my hand gets a slap along with the comment, "Get your hand off my bundle!"

Each of us has a tolerance for the number of cycles through the chain of reactions. When we reach our tolerance, depression begins to set in. If these cyclings are allowed to continue then the depression becomes worse.

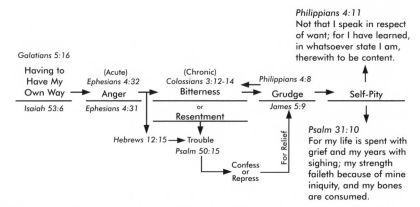

This verse appears above self pity in the diagram:

Not that I am implying that I was in any personal want, for I have learned how to be content (satisfied to the point where I am not disturbed or disquieted) in whatever state I am. Philippians 4:11 AMP

This statement was made by the apostle Paul and certainly doesn't sound like someone who feels sorry for himself.

Here then is the finished diagram of the Chain Reaction:

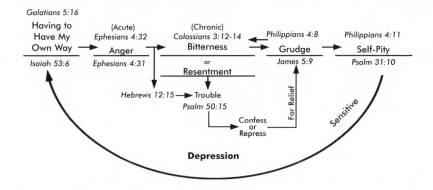

CHAPTER EIGHT

HOW CAN YOU BE FREE OF DEPRESSION?

Years ago I ask the Lord to give me a good illustration to be able to communicate the Biblical principle involved in coming out of depression. He did and it is, "Shifting Gears." Most everyone is familiar with shifting gears in a car.

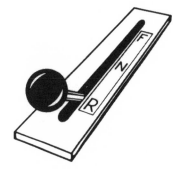

The diagram shows the three different gear positions.
> R = reverse
> N = neutral
> F = forward

In Reverse

Notice in the first diagram the gear shift is shown in reverse. Being in reverse represents unconfessed sin in the life. Once you are aware of the sin and do nothing about it, then you start going backward in your relationship with God. This then affects my relationship with those around me. Relationships also begin to go in reverse.

Once you are aware of this, hopefully you will remember to shift gears. How often do you shift gears? As often as you are aware of sin in your life! There are 2 steps in shifting gears,

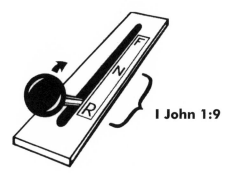

I John 1:9

Reverse to Neutral

The second diagram shows a bracket between reverse and neutral. The first step is to shift from reverse to neutral. This is done by confessing your sin. When you are convicted of anger then use the gear shift to confess your anger and disappointment (having to have my way). This will allow you to interrupt the chain reaction and you won't go further. The bracket points to I John 1:9, "If you confess your sins, He is faithful and just to forgive us our sins, and to cleanse us from all unrighteousness." Confession means to agree with God or call it the same thing. When you do, there are two things God does. He forgives and cleanses. The forgiveness restores fellowship with God. Cleansing means that God removes the sin. It is not there anymore.

When emotional damage has been done, confession is not the healing itself, rather it is the cleansing that allows the healing forces to begin their work. This would also be true in negative physical changes that might have occurred due to the tolerance of unconfessed sin.

Feelings

It has been said that all too often logic pales in the face of emotion.

Some have asked, "What if you don't feel like it is gone?" Many times our feelings can deceive us. If you don't feel different emotionally, then I would encourage you to follow through with step two and get into forward. Then remember that God's promise is more reliable than my feelings. Don't let your feelings rob you of what God wants to do for you. Continue to practice shifting gears and God will change the way you feel.

If you don't feel like the sin is gone due to some discomfort for physical reasons, then again you will need to be patient. Anyone who has remained in reverse for a period of time may have physical and physiological changes in the body. These changes, assuming they are reversible, may take a period of time to return to normal. Some of these changes may be irreversible. If so then you need to ask the Lord to keep you emotionally/spiritually comfortable as you bear this physical and/or physiological discomfort. More is said about this in Chapter Seven.

Matthew 12:43-45

I John 1:9

Clean and Empty

Taking the first step in shifting gears has taken you to neutral. Notice in the third diagram there is a reference to Mt. 12:43 - 45 KJV, "When the unclean spirit is gone out of a man, he walketh through dry places, seeking rest, and findeth none. Then he saith, I will return into my house from whence I came out; and when he is come, he findeth it empty, swept, and garnished. Then goeth he, and taketh with himself seven other spirits more wicked than himself, and they enter in and dwell there: and the last state of that man is worse than the first..."

Two things can be said about being in neutral. You are (1) clean and (2) empty. It is good to be clean but it is risky to be empty!!

This is a principle Jesus is making in the Matthew reference. I am not talking about demon possession. I am using these verses to illustrate the danger of remaining empty. Anyone who stops in neutral (clean and empty) will soon find themselves, as Jesus said, in worse condition than before. This is due to constantly falling back into reverse.

With this warning hopefully you won't stop or even pause in neutral. Step #2 must be taken to complete the gear shifting.

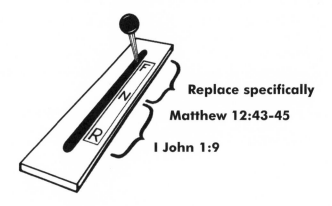

Replace specifically

Matthew 12:43-45

I John 1:9

Be Specific

The fourth diagram shows a bracket between neutral (N) and forward (F). In order to go from N to F you need to "replace specifically." This means you need to put something in this clean and empty space. I am recommending that you be specific in two areas.

First, be specific about what you ask the Lord to put in the empty space. The works of the flesh list contains sins we could use to confess from in going from R to N. The fruit of the Spirit list gives some good things for replacement. Secondly, be specific and ask for these replacements for the person or circumstances for which they are needed.

For example:

Confess - R to N	**Replace- N to F**
1. Lord, I am angry at my wife.	1. Give me love for my wife.
2. Lord, I am impatient with my wife.	2. Give me patience with my wife.

In my own life and in seeking to help others, I have found anger and impatience to be the most common responses when things don't go my way. That is why they are used in the example.

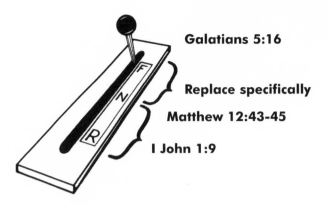

Galatians 5:16

Replace specifically

Matthew 12:43-45

I John 1:9

Prevention

After exercising step two you will find yourself in forward. The fifth diagram shows the Gal.5:16 reference beside it. This is one of the most important promises for a Christian found in the Bible.

This I say then, Walk in the Spirit and ye shall not fulfill the desires of the flesh. Gal. 5:16 KJV

The promise: If you choose to walk with the Holy Spirit in control of your life, then the desires, works of the flesh will not be manifest. Or to paraphrase using the gear shift illustration, the more you stay in forward the less you will find yourself in reverse. If you will quickly shift gears when necessary then you will find yourself in reverse less and less and less. Staying in forward and recovering back into forward will have some exciting results. You will have the possibility and the potential of not responding the same way you did the last time the same thing happened to you. You may fail and need to shift gears a number of times in regard to a recurring circumstance. Don't quit! The day will come when you will see the Holy Spirit prevent the wrong reactions. BE PATIENT!!

Be persistent until consistent!!

Observe the postage stamp: its usefulness depends upon its ability to stick to one thing until it gets there !

Each time you need to shift gears don't stop short of reaching forward. The warning: THERE IS NO PREVENTION IN NEUTRAL — to keep from slipping back into reverse.

Backsliding

Since I am using the gear shift in a car for this illustration, I want to use the car to stress the warning. We all know that life is uphill and the Christian life is no different.

When your car is on a hill in neutral what happens? It begins to roll backward. What could you do to stop rolling backward?

We know that the power is in the gas tank. So the obvious solution is to depress the gas pedal. But what happens to the car on a hill rolling backward and you depress the gas pedal? It might come as a surprise, but the car continues to roll backward! This is what happens to us in our spiritual lives. When we are aware that we are sliding backwards, we know that the power of God is available to us through the Holy Spirit. We cry out to God for His power to stop the slide. Many have been counseled to do this by well meaning friends. Certainly I would recommend asking God for His power but if you are still in "neutral", I don't believe it will be of value. In using the car in this illustration and analogy, the principle holds true , both for the car and for our spiritual walk. The car will only go up the hill when the gear shift is placed in forward.

The same is true in our spiritual life. It is critical that we go into "forward gear". When the gas pedal is depressed while the car is in forward gear, it will not only cease its backward slide, but will go uphill! The power in the gas tank can only be harnessed when the gear shift is in forward.

Just so, in our spiritual life the power of the Holy Spirit will only be harnessed when we are in forward gear.

Whenever we remain in reverse, stop in neutral, or are sliding backward, we will be caught up with our three enemies, the world the flesh and the devil. Yet when we are in forward and walking under the control of the Holy Spirit, we will have the power to go against our three enemies.

Let me repeat the admonition:
BEWARE THERE IS NO PREVENTION IN NEUTRAL!

Put Off and Put On

Be Specific

I have talked about reactions thus far in our illustrations. However, the principle of shifting gears needs to be used wherever wrong, sinful actions are involved. You may wonder where the gear shift principle is found in the Bible. You will find it scattered throughout both the old and the new testament. Possibly the clearest text is found in the last parts of the fourth chapter of Ephesians and the third chapter of Colossians.

The apostle Paul uses the words, "put off" and "put on" to communicate this principle. For example, look at Ephesians 4:31,32 KJV, "Let all bitterness and wrath, and anger, and clamour, and evil speaking, be put away from you with all malice: And be ye kind one to another, tenderhearted, forgiving one another, even as God for Christ's sake hath forgiven you."

Here Paul tells us to put away (put off):
1. bitterness
2. wrath
3. anger
4. clamour (any loud disturbance or noise)
5. evil speaking
6. malice (ill will; hostile)

Then *immediately* he tells us to be (put on):
1. kind
2. tender hearted
3. forgiving

In verses 22 and 24 he actually uses the words put off and put on.

Please notice that he named some *specific* sins to put away. Then some *specific* things for replacement. It is critical that you see that Paul said there are two steps, not one or the other. Also notice that there is an order for the two steps. Always put off first then put on. In the gear shift R to N represents put off; N to F represents put on. Both here and in Col. 3 he gives a number of lists of things to put off and put on. The steps are of equal importance.

Two Traps

Another great benefit this gear shift illustration offers is in explaining two traps which Christians commonly find themselves.

First Trap

The first trap is stopping in neutral. Many people in the counseling room or after a conference will say, "I never have known that I was supposed to replace after confession."

I spoke in a church several years ago and taught these principles. Afterwards a man came to me and said, " I am an elder in this church and have been a Christian for twenty years. I have never heard of the need to replace after confession. When I saw him a week later he said, "I have been replacing and this has been the best week of my Christian life".

There are three possible explanations for not replacing:
1. Simply didn't know
2. Did know but forgot
3. Know but aren't willing

Breaking Old Habits

For those who know but forget, they need to form a habit of going on into forward. The old habit of stopping in neutral is difficult to break. Also it is common for some to view the replacement as not being very important. In second and third counseling appointments, when asked, "how are you doing", there is a typical response. They usually say, "I have been confessing my sin real often." This is often repeated several times in the conversation. I will point out that they did not mention the replacement (N to F). The response is, "I have been replacing, I just forgot to say it." I warn them that they need to view the replacement as important as the confession.

Someone has said:

Habits are first cobwebs, then cables.

It takes time to break cables. Be patient and faithful.
The Lord will enable you.

Not Willing

Those who know but are not willing to replace believe that the other person might benefit. If they remain in reverse harboring bitterness, it is difficult to ask the Lord to give them love or to cause their love to increase and abound toward the other person. This is especially true if they are blaming the other person for their discomfort.

My State is Worse

I want to continue with the story of the wife of the adulterous traveling salesman. You will recall that he was always anxious to get back to the "territory". Her story gives very clear evidence of the results of stopping in neutral and failing to go to forward gear.

She had come to see me because she was depressed. She had been taking an anti-depressant for several months. As we talked she was willing to admit that she was angry, bitter and jealous. We talked about shifting gears and she said she understood and would give it a try. I tried to communicate to her that when you come to the Lord for help , you don't present your husband, you present yourself!

Three appointments later she came in the door and said, "Dr.Peeples, my state is worse now than it was when I first came to see you." (Now that is a real encouragement for your counselor!) I asked her to turn in her Bible to Matthew 12:43,45 and read it to me. She said, "What does that have to do with me?" I asked her to reread verse 45 which says, "I tell you that man's state is worse now than at the beginning." I asked her to recall what she said upon entering the room. She seemed a little surprised that her words were the same as those she had just read. She asked me to explain. I suggested that we review the gear shift. She assured me that the Lord had convicted her of her sin and she had been confessing. But she said, I am not getting better. I commended her for her confession (going from R to F). Then I reminded her that she needed to go from N into F. She was not sure what I meant. (This was the third time I had gone over the gear shift illustration with her.)

She needed to replace her anger, bitterness and jealousy with love for her husband. She replied, "Are you suggesting that I love my husband after what he has done to me?" I said yes. As I watched the expression on her face, she became nauseous. The upper part of her body began to shake as her face contorted at the very suggestion that she love her husband. After she settled down she assured me that she could not do that! I knew that she could but she had decided that she wouldn't. Later on as she walked through the door to leave, I stopped her and asked her again to let the Lord give her love for her husband. Her reply, "No, I am not going to do that after the way he has treated me, he doesn't deserve it, he might benefit!"

Second Trap

The second trap is to try and start in neutral. By this I mean there is an attempt to skip confession (R to N). This is typically done because of the need for love, joy, peace and comfort. Today that is where the emphasis is. "Let's not talk about sin, I really want and need some peace and joy." To bring up the idea that sin maybe involved, is viewed as being negative. I am interested in the positive. However to try and take some joy and peace and "dump" it in on top of unconfessed sin won't work. The Bible speaks to this very clearly.

"He who covers his transgressions shall not prosper, but whoever confesses and forsakes his sins shall obtain mercy." Proverbs 28:13 AMP

To offer peace and joy to someone whose heart is heavy because of sin and not deal with the sin reminds me of Proverbs 25:20, "He who sings songs to a heavy heart is like him who lays off a garment in cold weather and as vinegar upon soda." Ungers Bible dictionary says that to pour vinegar upon soda, "results in a violet effervescence."
Always start with confession (R) and move through neutral (N) to forward (F)!
In summary remember the three positions in the gear shift:

"Shifting Gears"

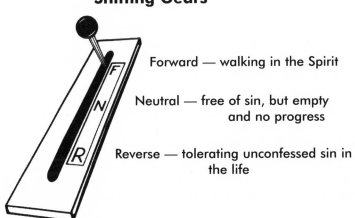

Forward — walking in the Spirit

Neutral — free of sin, but empty and no progress

Reverse — tolerating unconfessed sin in the life

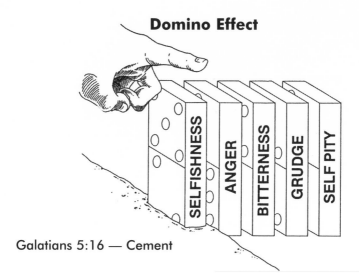

Domino Effect

Galatians 5:16 — Cement

The "Domino Effect" gives another means of understanding the Biblical principal presented in the gear shift. The picture shows a hand with a finger poised to thump the first domino. When the thump occurs, one falls against the other until all are down.

However you can interrupt the process by taking hold of the falling domino and prevent it from involving the next domino. Just so you can choose not to fail of the grace of God when you get angry by taking hold of the anger (domino) and prevent it from resulting in bitterness or resentment. By taking hold, I mean to do what the apostle Paul said do when he said, "Let all wrath, and bitterness and anger be put away from you...." (Eph. 4:31). The only way you can put away anger is to confess it as sin and experience God's forgiveness and cleansing. This is the first part of shifting gears (R-N). Then it is important to follow through by going into forward (N-F). In so doing you have yielded afresh to the control of the Holy Spirit. This "pours the cement" around the first domino (having to have my way). The cement represents the promise of Galatians 5:16, KJV "This I say then walk in the Spirit and you will not fulfill the desires of the flesh."

All of us get thumps in life. When you find that your response to the thump is anger, then discipline yourself to immediately shift gears. Then according to God's promise, when the cement continues to build up, the day will come when the same thump occurs, you will not have an angry response. I am not talking about perfection, I am simply referring back to the earlier statement when I said, "The more you stay in forward the less you will find yourself in reverse."

Karen's Story
Encouraging

The following story is exciting and encouraging for two reasons:

1. The principles shared in this book were shared with a 12 year old girl by a close friend who has practiced these principles for many years. Her confidence in the Lord's faithfulness enabled her to share with this young girl.

2. The principles were easily grasped and put into practice at age 12. Many have asked us about how early in life can someone understand and practice these Biblical principles. Her story should convince you to feel confident in sharing with young people.

Although Karen did not say she was depressed our friend felt that she was moving in that direction.

The problems listed below were written out and given to our friend.

I. I'm trying too hard to be perfect.
   A. I expect more of myself than is possible
   B. I put myself under too much pressure
II. I set goals too high for myself to reach
   A. Being a perfectionist I expect to meet my "out of league" goals
   B. I have a habit of looking around me and concentrating on how much can be done.
   C. If I start slacking on my goal, I push myself.
III. Life is changing fast for me
   A. In the last 3 years a lot has happened.
      1. mom's death
      2. physical changes
      3. mental changes
      4. spiritual changes

Our friend pointed out that her perfectionism was simply another way of saying that she lived a life of wanting and expecting her own way. Then she was asked to describe the responses that went on inside her when things didn't go her way. Our friend read and explained to her Proverbs

4:23 KJV, "Keep your heart with all diligence; for out of it are the issues of life." She saw that the issues in her life were not the problems she had listed, but her responses to them.

Our friend then shared the gear shift with her. It was amazing how quickly she understood and responded.

A day or two later Karen wrote the following and brought it to our friend.

Before you confess your sins, your heart is impure. Therefore God can't work in you because he can't even look at you heart. In this illustration, the cup is filled with dirty impure water with bacteria swimming in it, just as your heart is filled with sin before you confess.

When you confess, God takes the evil out of you heart. In this illustration, He pours the water out of the cup and rinses it out thoroughly.

After you confess, don't leave it empty!! An empty heart is more dangerous than a dirty heart. Instead you need to ask God to replace it with the fruit of the Spirit. In the illustration, God pours clean fresh pure water back into the cup.

**An important verse to remember:

> *"Keep your heart with all diligence:*
> *for out of it are the issues of life."*

The second page contained some verses Karen had studied and the way she used diagrams to explain her understanding.

THE KEY

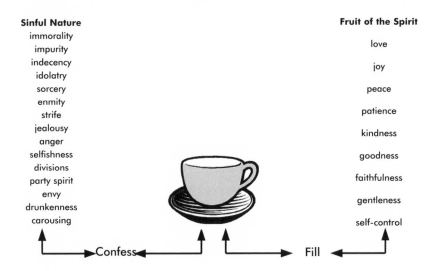

Sinful Nature
immorality
impurity
indecency
idolatry
sorcery
enmity
strife
jealousy
anger
selfishness
divisions
party spirit
envy
drunkenness
carousing

Fruit of the Spirit
love
joy
peace
patience
kindness
goodness
faithfulness
gentleness
self-control

Confess   Fill

The above lists came from Galatians 5:19-23 AMP

**confess - agree with God
**iniquity - having to have things your own way
**diligence - sticking with something; setting your mind to something

Another reminder:

Keep you heart with all diligence; for out of it are the issues of life.

Praise the Lord for such clear explanations! This should encourage us all to share with our children and our grandchildren at an early age.

What a difference my life would have been if I had started at the age of twelve and practiced these principles throughout my life!

Sue's Story

"Praise the Lord, O my soul and forget not all his benefits who forgives all your sins and heals all your diseases, who redeems your life from the pit and crowns you with love and compassion, who satisfies your desires with good things so that your youth is renewed like the eagles." Psalm 103

Dear Sam and Mary Glynn,

I enjoyed talking with you on the phone. I have been thinking how to start writing what God has done and this verse seemed appropriate.

I remember you telling us at the conference that we were not there for a mountain top experience but rather a valley one. I guess that was pretty much true because the weekend was heart rending. I went expecting, needing some answers for my life. I was ready to accept what was offered. Thank God you came bringing the truth. I told you on the phone, that even a valley experience is up from being in the pit. It is like I am out of the grave. Thank you, Jesus!

It is good to be free from the anger, bitterness and self-pity, that has controlled my life. I could not even identify it. It is hard for me to understand how I was so blind to something so simple.

Many years and many thousands of dollars have been spent trying to figure out what was wrong with me. The story is so long and repetitive I don't look forward to penning it.

I have spent most of my life looking for love and attention from other people. My first overdose was at 14. I was hospitalized for three months in a psychiatric ward. Since then I have been hospitalized several times for addiction, harm to myself, anxiety or depression. At least 6 times that I can count, probably more. I was hospitalized 2 years ago in a mental hospital for severe anxiety, chronic depression and labeled severely neurotic. I was told to expect a life of depression and defeat.

There are too many details, doctors and circumstances for me to write, but the result of much money, counseling and time brought heartache and damage and brokenness for me and my family.

I accepted Jesus as my Saviour at a young age during a youth crusade. I grew up in a strong Christian home. I knew the Lord, I just never allowed Him to clean my heart. I thought everybody else had made me the way I was.

My mom and biological Dad divorced when I was 3 or 4. He had serious problems and was arrested several times. Mom married and her husband adopted my older brother and me. He brought us to the town where I grew up.

My Dad is a prominent well respected business man. I grew up with many advantages. I did not have any monetary needs but I remember stealing at the age of 5. I continued this pattern. I was already acting out of anger. Though I came from an affluent family with a strong Christian heritage, I never learned how to forgive. I was introduced to sex at a very early age and lived promiscuously looking for love and fulfillment.

It is difficult to remember how desperate I have been but not so difficult because I have been redeemed. One of the main lessons I have learned is to not allow myself to focus on my past and what has happened to me but to pay attention to my reactions. I am very thankful for His mercy, for His forgiveness, for the Word.

Thank you for your ministry. I know God has used you in many lives and will continue. I know also He saved me through what I have learned. It has been like a heart transplant. He took my heart full of disease (sin), cleansed it and made the same heart healthy. I want to keep it that way. Proverbs 4:23, Keep your heart with all diligence for out of it are the issues of life.

God bless you,
Sue

She sent me three pages of computer print out of 6 months of prescription drugs for her "mental illness." The total cost was $546.00. She also sent me copies of two MMPT (Minnesota Multiphasic Personality Inventory) evaluations. These are psychological instruments used to assess a persons mental and emotional condition. They were taken 16 months apart. One was before she came to the conference and began to work through the notebook, Applying Truth to Life (written by Mary Glynn and two of her friends.) The improvement was so great that she asked to retake the evaluation. The therapist was reluctant because in his opinion, being only 16 months apart, there would not be any significant difference.

These are some of the evaluation remarks from the first report:
1) Intense anger, hostility, resentment and would like to get back at those responsible for her condition.
2) Overwhelmed by anxiety, tension and depression. Feels helpless and alone, inadequate and insecure. Believes life is hopeless.
3) Preoccupied with feeling guilty and unworthy. Feels she needs to be punished for wrongs she has done.
4) Feels hopeless at times and is a condemned person.
5) Low self esteem

6) Immobilized, withdrawn and no energy for life

Resulting labels:
1) Severely neurotic
2) Anxiety Disorder
3) Dysmythmic Disorder in a Schizoid Personality
4) Schizophrenic Disorder should also be considered

Recommended treatment:
1) Intensive psychological treatment
2) Psychotropic medications
3) Individuals with this profile present a clear suicide risk; precaution should be taken.

Sixteen months later after repeating the same MMPI evaluation:
1) Patient's self esteem is very good
2) Absence of depressive and anxiety feelings
3) Her addictive personality from the past shows significant psychological gain.
4) A good score on ego strength shows she can stand up and take care of herself.
5) Appears able to relate well with others and is quite confident in her ability to do so.
6) Given where she was 16 months ago, it appears she is making excellent progress.

In his conversation with her, he was amazed that a change of this magnitude could take place in such a short period of time. "Borders on the miraculous", was his comment.

This second evaluation was done three years ago. I have talked with Sue on the phone recently and she continues to be consistent in her spiritual, mental and emotional stability. All of the credit for the change and consistency she gives to the Lord!!

Sue decided to take the Lord at His Word and trust Him to do that which He promised. I am reminded of the statement concerning Mary, the mother of our Saviour, in Luke 1:45 KJV "And blessed is she that believed; for there shall be a performance of those things which were told her from the Lord."

I have included a great deal of detail in Sue's life long story because in most cases this story would be viewed as far too serious and complicated for Biblical counseling alone!! Or since she "only" trusted in the Lord and

His Word, she must not have been as depressed as was originally diagnosed! However, we see that through repentance, confession, faith and a yielding to the Holy Spirit's control, she was able to see dramatic changes!

Sue's information and instruction came by way of a conference, studying her Bible with the aid of a devotional notebook and several long distance phone calls.

For the Word of God is quick and powerful and sharper than any two edged sword, piercing even to the dividing asunder of soul and spirit, and of the joints and marrow and is a discerner of the thoughts and intents of the heart. Hebrews 43:12 KJV

Will you let the Word of God be quick, powerful and discerning for you? We trust that Sue's powerful testimony will encourage you. Remember that, "God is not a respecter of persons" and that what He has and is doing for Sue, He is waiting and willing to do for you.

Susan's Story
God's Providence

Susan shared her story over the phone of how the Lord had worked in her life. I asked her to write her story so that others might benefit from her experience. She was happy to do so. The following is her letter that was written almost two years ago.

I became a Christian when I was five years old and from that point forward I have never doubted that Jesus entered my heart. Yet despite my sincere conversion I was a terribly unhappy child, pouting most of the time and suffering from a very low self image. I struggled with bitterness and resentment throughout my childhood, teen years and twenties. During high school, college and the years immediately following I had everything the world considers important for happiness: beauty, talents, friends, boyfriends, money, many awards for musical and dramatic talents and sports ability. Still, I was unhappy, increasingly depressed and suffering from a very low self image. I held on to a firm belief that the Bible contained ALL the answers to overcome my difficulties. Yet, no matter how much I studied my Bible, prayed and read Christian books I could not seem to unlock the proper Biblical principles to relieve my pain and unhappiness!

For many years my depression was so severe that I cried out to God in anger for ever creating me. I dreamed of committing suicide and the different ways I might do it painlessly or so it would look like an accident. Having Jesus in my heart, I knew this was not the answer but I felt desperate and helpless. I wanted relief! During my early thirties a friend invited me to a women's ministry banquet at our church. At this function I won a prize, Mary Glynn Peeples' Successful Stress Management seminar tapes. I have never before nor have I since been to one of these women's ministry functions and I am convinced that God sent me there to receive these tapes in answer to my cries for help.

Since listening to and applying the Biblical principles in those tapes approximately six years ago, I have not suffered from any depression other than one day of crisis. This day came after my two small children and I had been sick for over six weeks and I had only had about three hours sleep a night. At my point of desperation my husband realized my severe fatigue and took care of the children. I had a heartfelt prayer time and a good night's sleep and I was fine from that point forward. The many years free from depression and a low self esteem are proof enough that these principles work!

The first and most important principle I learned is that depression is just a big pout. An adult form of pouting that sounds acceptable instead of pure self-centeredness. This freed me to see how silly and selfish I was being. I realized my depression simply came from "having to have my own way" (Isa. 53:6) and I was able to confess my sin and get on with my life FREE from depression!!

Another principle and verse which has helped me is the gear shift principle of sin being reverse, confession and cleansing being neutral and asking God to fill the void with the fruits of the Spirit being forward. I apply this principle daily as well as pray that God will cause my love to increase and abound for all people (Phil 1:9-11; I Thes.3:12) I have found if I do this daily I am content, joyful and much more loving.

After hearing that a low self image comes from refusing instruction, (He that refuseth instruction despiseth his own soul

Proverbs 15:32a KJV) which by the way, I remember doing since I was at least six or seven — I have been able to confess my self-centered attitude and other sins, and I have had a healthy self image ever since! (He that getteth wisdom loveth his own soul Proverbs 19:8a KJV)

After hearing how to apply Bible verses such as "perfect love casts out fear"(I John 4:18) I was able to live alone in our house for three months while my husband was out of the country without the fear I had so struggled with in the past. Before, if he left for just one night I could not sleep because of my terrible fears.

Understanding how to apply Bible verses in my life and the principles based on the Bible taught by the Peeples has literally saved me from a life of unhappiness and depression. I am unendingly indebted to them and to God who provided the wisdom they shared with me. I review the material at least every six months to keep on track. I have not found any information before or since that has helped me so tremendously as the information they share. God's Word works!!

I appreciate the opportunity to share my story. God has blessed me and continues to bless others as I share this information with them!

Love in Christ,
Susan

What an encouragement to us! Not only is she consistently better personally but she is reaching out and helping others!

CHAPTER NINE

JONAH AND HIS DEPRESSION

As I studied the Bible seeking an understanding about depression, I asked the Lord to lead me to a character in the Bible that would clearly demonstrate the principles illustrated in the Chain Reaction. I looked at several characters that I thought would be appropriate. When I considered Jonah, there was my answer. He clearly followed through the steps in the Chain Reaction without having to fabricate or force anything into the story.

Wrong Direction

As we walk through the book of Jonah, we will follow his story. Unless otherwise stated the verses quoted are from the Living Bible. In verses 1 and 2, the Lord told Jonah to get up and go to the city of Ninevah. God gave Jonah the message he was to deliver to the people. In verse 3, we see Jonah's response. He was afraid and decided to run away. He proceeded to the port of Joppa and found a ship leaving for Tarshish. The King James Version of the Bible says that he paid the price for the ticket and boarded the ship. Reading the story further, we discover exactly what "price he paid"! Ninevah was inland to the north east of the Tigris River. Tarshish was across the Mediterranean Sea, up the Atlantic coast of Spain. Tarshish was in the opposite direction from Ninevah! Tarshish was at the end of the known world. Surely if Jonah could reach the end of the world, God would not find him. Actually he planned to hide before the ship ever left port. At the end of verse 3 we read, "he climbed down into the dark hold of the ship to hide there from the Lord."

Stormy Weather

When the ship was out at sea, a great storm arose and the men feared for their lives. In desperation, the sailors began to call out to their gods for help. The captain told Jonah to get up, cry out to his god and find out if he would have mercy and save them.

The next solution involved drawing straws to see who was responsible for the storm. Even the heathen sailors believed there were consequences for disobedience! Don't see much of that today, even among Christians!

Jonah was questioned and then asked, "What should we do to you to stop the storm?" The storm was getting worse and worse. Jonah's response was for them to throw him into the sea because "this terrible storm has come because of me." Jonah is finally realizing the consequences of his sin of selfishness, wanting to go his own way — to Tarshish!

Further efforts to row ashore failed and the crew cried out to Jonah's God, Jehovah. They asked that they not die because of Jonah's sin. They threw Jonah into the raging sea and the storm stopped! The men were awestruck.

A Whale of a Story

In verse 17 we read that the Lord had arranged for a great fish to swallow Jonah. He was inside this fish for 3 days and 3 nights.

Chapter 2 opens with Jonah praying from inside the fish. The first part of the prayer deals with his description of what he experienced as he was descending to the depths of the sea. Like so many of us, when we are in the storms of life, he started making promises. In verse 9 he said, "I will surely fulfill my promises." Then the prayer ends with, "For my deliverance comes from the Lord alone." I believe the deliverance he was referring to was from the fish. But what about deliverance from his selfishness, fear, and the disobedience of running and hiding? These are not mentioned in his prayer. There is no confession of sin. This may seem a minor detail but the results of his not dealing with this sin will soon become evident.

Verse 10 tells us that the Lord ordered the fish to spit up Jonah on the beach. The fish was more obedient than Jonah! He spit him up! In the book of Revelation chapter 3 verse 16, God spoke to the church at Ladoicea, "I know you well — you are neither hot or cold; I wish you were one or the other! But since you are merely lukewarm, I will spit you out of my mouth!" I believe Jonah was lukewarm and the fish spit him out. This could be the description of the average Christian. And the problem with the average Christian is that he is just an average Christian.

Right Direction

Chapter 3 opens with Jonah on dry land again. The Lord spoke and repeated His orders. Verse 3 tells us that Jonah obeyed but I wonder what his spirit was like? As we continue in the story we will find out. Jonah turned and went to Nineveh. This was a large city. It would take three days to walk around it. The first day in the city, Jonah began to preach and the people repented. He preached that Nineveh would be destroyed in 40 days. This was the message God had given him to deliver to this wicked city. What does it mean to repent? The dictionary's definition: "to remember with sorrow; to change your mind; to change your course." From the king to the lowest peasant, the people declared a fast. They put on sackcloth and sat in ashes. The animals were denied food and water. The message was sent throughout the city to cry out to God and turn from their evil ways.

A very interesting and important truth is learned from verse 10. "And when God saw that they had put a stop to their evil ways, He abandoned His plan to destroy them." What is the basis of God's decision? Was it the fasting, the sackcloth, the ashes and the crying? No! We are told it was because they put a stop to their evil ways! What a lesson for us, what a lesson for our nation!

Murmuring

What was Jonah's response when God changed His mind? Chapter 4 opens with Jonah's response; he was angry! Now we have written evidence that Jonah was in step 2 of the Chain Reaction. He must have been angry long before he reached Nineveh. However this is the first record we have of his problem.

Jonah begins to complain to the Lord and starts reviewing the immediate past. Jonah is playing his "grudge tapes." As you listen to the story, there seems to be bitterness and resentment in his heart. The people in Nineveh had been so evil and now they were in a state of repentance. Jonah was not happy over God's decision to change His mind. Jonah wanted these people to pay for what they had done! Notice how Jonah proceeded though the Chain Reaction. He was not getting his way (step 1), he was angry (step 2), his anger became bitterness/resentment (step 3), played his grudge tapes (step 4) and he felt sorry for himself (step 5). He defended, justified and rationalized his behavior as he played his "grudge tape" before God! In verse 3 of chapter 4 Jonah has become depressed. He declares, "Please kill me, Lord. I'd rather be dead than alive." Jonah had told the people that God was going to destroy the city in 40 days. Now God changed his mind. What would the people think of Jonah when they found that his prophesied warning was not going to happen. Jonah was completely absorbed in himself, filled with self pity . What will these people think of me? What will the people back home think of me?

Pity Party

In verse 4 God challenges him about his anger. "Is it right to be angry about this?" Jonah's response: he went out and sat sulking on the east side of the city. Jonah is having a "pity party". Poor me, woe is me. He constructed a leafy shelter to shade him from the sun as he waited to see if the city would be destroyed. Jonah was sensitive to the sun!!Jonah has now completed the cycle through the Chain Reaction and is headed for another cycle. Surely this was not his first cycle, but it is the first one we can document.

The leaves of Jonah's shelter withered in the heat. God's second arrangement for Jonah comes into view. "The Lord arranged for a vine to grow up quickly and to spread its broad leaves over Jonah's head to shade him. This made him comfortable and very grateful." Jonah is finding his comfort in the creation not the Creator! Risky! Why? Keep reading.

Verse 7, "But God also prepared a worm! The next morning, the worm ate through the stem of the plant and it withered and died." Now we have had 2 arrangements and 1 preparation.

Jonah sat under the hot sun. God ordered a scorching east wind to blow on Jonah. He grew faint and wished for death.(In the beginning of the book statistics were quoted of the people who commit suicide, most are depressed.) The hot sun and the scorching wind revealed his sensitivity. In this state of mind (filled with self-pity) he again stated, "Death is better than this." God challenged him a second time about his anger, "Is it right for you to be angry because the plant died?"

Anger Defended

"Yes" Jonah said, "it is right for me to be angry enough to die!" Again we see a spirit of defensiveness and justification. Remember the best selling book mentioned earlier, written by a well known physician entitled,

"Your Anger Can Kill You." Jonah, even in his day, had enough insight to know that if he accumulated enough anger he would die! Few Christians take seriously the effects of anger, both spiritually, emotionally and physically.

In verse 10 the Lord said to Jonah, "You feel sorry for yourself." Then God warns him of finding comfort in the shelter (the creation). "You did no work to put it there and it is, at best, short lived."

Right Place — Wrong Spirit

In the last verse, God stated His right to feel sorry for the city of Ninevah, 120,000 people in spiritual darkness. God's messenger finally got to the right destination and proclaimed the right message. But what was the spiritual and emotional state of the messenger? As we have and will find out — not so good!

Jonah's failure to interrupt his moving down through the Chain Reaction left him in bad shape. He could not handle the events of the day, especially when it did not go his way! God had His way but Jonah did not have his!

The story of God's prophet, Jonah, ends with him on a hillside; angry, bitter, resentful, grudge bearing, defensive, feeling sorry for himself, sensitive and depressed.

Sad Ending

What a way to end a life! What an unnecessary way to end a life! The fourth question we want to answer for you so you won't forget: how to get out of depression? You may find yourself in a hot seat with no place to hide. You may find yourself in the midst of a hot east wind but you don't have to live in spiritual darkness. The condition of your heart determines how you handle the "hot spots" of life.

God has provided a way for us to be enlightened. The Bible clearly teaches how to avoid depression. It is the result of sin. When we do not get our way, our natural tendency is to become angry. Remember I John 1:9 teaches us to confess and be forgiven and cleansed. When God cleanses us we are empty and it is important that we ask to be filled with the Holy Spirit.

Lessons to be Learned

We learn many great lessons from the book of Jonah. One great lesson is the answer to our fourth question: how can you prevent becoming depressed?

The answer to this question is to walk in the Spirit. This walk means there is no unconfessed sin in your life, the Holy spirit is controlling your life and selfishness is under His control. This walk is maintained as you quickly confess your sin (put it away) and replace it (put on) with the fruit of the Spirit (shifting gear). As you continue this walk you will find that you still continue to sin but you sin less and less. As you choose to deny the self life and be controlled by the Spirit, the need to put away and put on will be less and less. This is a promise made to us from God in Gal. 5:16 KJV, "This I say then walk in the spirit and you will not fulfill the desires of the flesh."

I am not sure how to title this story. Should it be; A Fishy Sheep Story or a Sheepish Fish Story? Which would you choose?

My prayer is that God will seal in our hearts these lessons from Jonah and in His love and grace bring them to our minds that we may glorify our Lord and enjoy more and more our walk with Him.

Chain Reaction
Jonah's Depression

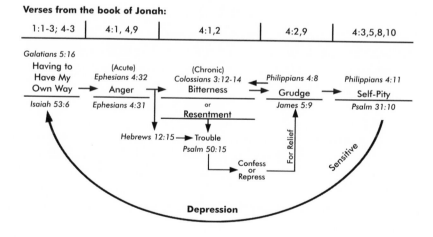

10

HOW CAN YOU PREVENT DEPRESSION?

Since the accumulation of cycles through the Chain Reaction brings on depression, our goal is to learn how to stop the flow through the Chain Reaction. If we interrupt the flow between the reactions, then a cycle is avoided. If it is avoided, then obviously no accumulation of cycles can occur.

How to Interrupt the Flow

The gear shift principle is used to interrupt the flow.
The following diagrams will make the application clear.

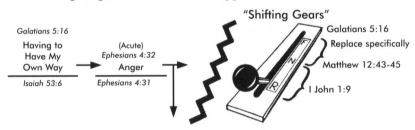

Regardless of where you find yourself in the Chain Reaction stop and use the gear shift. Hopefully you will interrupt the flow at anger each time.

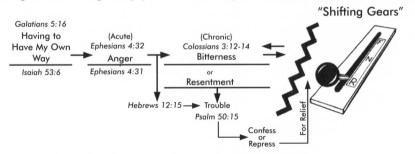

If you find yourself bitter, then use the gear shift there.

If you catch yourself playing one of your grudge video tapes, quickly shift gears.

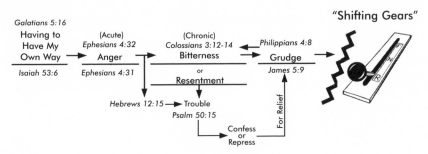

Should you get down to self pity, hopefully you will shift gears before you have a pity party!

Another reminder: always end up in forward gear! Only in forward will God's great promise of Galatians 5:16 be yours: Stay in forward gear and you will find yourself in reverse less and less!

This protection is of vital importance because we are like tea bags and will never know how strong we are until we are in hot water.

Your "hot water" may be just around the corner!

The Bank

How quick does it take to cycle through this Chain Reaction? Are we talking about minutes, hours, days, weeks? It may not take as long as you think. I was coming back to the office one day after lunch. Had a one o'clock counseling appointment. I needed to go by the bank and make a deposit. My office is six minutes from the bank. It was fifteen minutes to one, so I had time to take care of my banking and meet my appointment.

To enter the teller area you drive through a one way, one lane wide drive way. You come through this drive and pull into an area with four teller lanes. Great day, good lunch, just coming in to make a deposit. Suddenly, I stopped at the entrance because a car was blocking the entrance. I waited for this car to move into one of the four lanes. Three of the teller windows were open but no cars were there.

A lady was sitting in the car blocking the teller lanes. I was ready to get out and help her. I assumed her car had stalled. It was summer time and the windows were down in my car. I looked and there were fumes coming out of the tail pipe in the lady's car. I knew then her car was running. I wondered why she had decided to stop and block the traffic. I looked and saw cars lining up behind me. Horns began to sound. I was the car directly behind this lady. I was afraid she could not hear the car horns behind me. I decided to assist these impatient bank customers by blowing my horn. Each time I blew my horn, her brake lights got brighter. I could see her knee locked against the brake pedal!

I have an investigative mind and I decided to try to find out what is happening. There are about fifteen parking spaces on the side of the lane. All the spaces were filled. She chose to block the lane while waiting to park her car. There were many places in the area for her to wait rather than blocking the entrance.

I was ready to open my car door when a man from a car behind me walked by. He went to her car and pressed his face against her window. She refused to look at him. She starred straight ahead. He came back shaking his head from side to side. I closed my door. I saw what he found. Why should I go look?

Beside Myself

Now I am almost "beside myself!" Not angry, "just beside myself!" It seemed many minutes later before she moved her car. A parking space finally opened for her. She slowly drove her car into this space. Horns were still blowing and now the tellers were looking out of their windows trying to see what was happening.

I arrived at one of the tellers first! I was "upset". I lowered the window in my car and threw my deposit to the teller. I looked into the rear view mirror and saw her with her purse under her arm, "prancing" through the parking lot. I wanted to put my car in reverse. I had my foot over the accelerator when I realized there was another car behind me.

I have banked here for many years. Beside all four of those teller windows, are signs which read, "No left turn." Guess which way to my office! I am late for an appointment to help someone with their disobedience. I looked to see if there was a car with a blue light on top. There wasn't, so the Christian Biblical Counselor turned left.

I am going up a hill to my office. I see bright red brake lights fixed in the windshield of my car. I am saying, "that idiotic, stupid, inconsiderate female"! I never saw anything like that. Now I am late and I will be behind my schedule all afternoon.

As I pulled up in front of my office I was mumbling to myself and continuing to review the scene at the bank. I was talking to myself. As I opened the door to my car I said, "Wait a minute, what is going on." I did not want that lady to park there and she should not have parked there. It was O.K. for me to get angry. Right? We have all been behind a lady like that.

Was it right for me to be angry? Did the Apostle Paul really mean all when he said to put away all anger? I was bitter before I knew it. All the way back to my office I played my grudge tape. I was mumbling to myself and filled with self pity. What did I realize I needed to do? I needed to shift gears. In prayer I confessed, "Lord, I am angry, bitter, impatient, bearing a grudge and feeling sorry for myself." I thanked Him for forgiving and cleansing me. Then I asked Him to give me love and patience for the little old lady at the bank! I needed this protection because I might be stopped behind her again.

This took place in a time frame of about fifteen minutes. I had completed one cycle of the Chain Reaction. If I had not interrupted this, I would have completed one cycle and in my "sensitive" state it would have been easier to add another cycle. This can be subtle so never ignore your reactions when things don't go your way.

Walking in the Spirit

This is obviously the essential need if you are going remain in fellowship with the Lord. Walking in the Spirit will prevent you from slipping back into depression.

Most Christians when asked what is involved in walking in the Spirit have answered:

> Praying regularly
> Bible reading and study
> Witnessing
> Having a quiet time
> Tithing
> Helping others

Surely you are aware that you can do some or all of the above and not walk in the Spirit. The definition of walking in the Spirit is self explanatory. It simply means that as you walk through the day, the Holy

Spirit is in control of your life.

Often when a Christian is aware that they are not where they ought to be spiritually, there is an attempt to, "double up", in their efforts in some or all of the items in the above list. Every thing in the list is vitally important to the Christian life.

All of the items in the list God wants us to do as SUPPLEMENTS to walking in the Spirit, but not to use them as a SUBSTITUTE!!

We emphasize this to help you avoid the trap of using that which is supplemental as a substitute for walking in the Spirit.

What we do in our Christian life is very important. But God's purpose is to transform us in order to "be" what He wants us to "be". (Romans 8:28-29) What we do should be a direct reflection of what we are.

When we are not a reflection of what we are, we are hypocrites. Hypocrite is a Greek word used to describe an actor. In the classical Greek theater, the actors wore masks. They had two faces, the one the audience saw and the real one underneath the mask.

Your walk begins with the desire to submit your body as a living sacrifice to God. This desire comes from an intellectual understanding of who God is and motivated by what He has done for us. This is the greatest point of resistance because it involves change. Man does not want to change. In order to start your walk in the Spirit, you must overcome this resistance and submit yourself to God.

God's Grace

All of this is available to us because of the grace of God. Grace is God's unmerited favor toward us. We don't deserve it but because of His mercy and love, He extends it to us. It has accurately been described as, " God's beneficent work for us, wholly independent of what we are and what we do. It is not merely God's attitude toward us but His activity in our behalf."

Socrates said, "The way to gain a good reputation is to endeavor to be what you desire to appear."

Daily homework: Constantly watch how you react or respond when things don't go the way you want them to.

CHAPTER ELEVEN

GOD'S LOVE — AN ABSOLUTE NECESSITY

Eagerly pursue and seek to acquire (this) love — make it your aim, your great quest:....I Cor. 14:1a AMP

Above all things have intense and unfailing love for one another, for love covers a multitude of sins — forgives and disregards the offenses of others. I Peter 4:8 AMP

There is no question about love being the key word in the Bible. Each author of the New Testament understood the practical significance of its emphasis. All my Christian life, I clearly saw the emphasis but only about 15 years ago did I understand the absolute necessity of making love my greatest aim and quest in life.

An "Is" Word

Love is the first part of the fruit of the Spirit. It is the only part that has 20 components or characteristics. As you examine these components, it is easy to see their absolute practical application. This is true for all of life. It also has specific application to the Chain Reaction leading to depression.

As you look at the opening words of the fourth verse of I Cor. 13 leading to the 20 components it says "Love is"....

Notice here that love is an "is" word. This is true most of the times it appears in the New Testament. Our misunderstanding comes because we automatically think of love as a "do" word. In other words if you love someone, to prove it or demonstrate it, you must do something for them.

God wants us to be a loving person and the measurement of whether we are or not is found in the list of the 20 components. You can do loving things and not be a Christian. However, you can't be a loving person without the Holy Spirit in your life and in control!

Here are the 20 components/characteristics:

1.	suffers long and is kind	11.	is not touchy
2.	never jealous	12.	does not hold grudges
3.	never envious	13.	hardly even notices when others do it wrong
4.	never boastful		
5.	never proud	14.	never glad about injustices
6.	never haughty	15.	rejoices when truth wins
7.	never selfish	16.	bears all things
8.	never rude	17.	believes all things
9.	does not demand its own way	18.	hopes all things
		19.	endures all things
10.	is not irritable	20.	never fails

(This list is a compilation taken from the Living Bible and the King James Version.)

We read in I Thes. 3:12, "And may the Lord make you to increase and excel and overflow in love for one another and for all people, just as we also do for you." AMP

Here we are admonished to ask the Lord not only to love but to see that love increases and excels toward all people.

Protection

If we are obedient to do this, how will it help in escaping and preventing depression? When shifting gears to escape depression, remember to replace specifically when you go from neutral to forward. As you leave neutral to go to forward always start with love as the first replacement. There are two specific scriptures that speak to the reason for doing this.

"Hatred stirreth up strife; but love covereth all sins." Proverbs 10:12 KJV

"Above all things have intense and unfailing love for one another, for love covers a multitude of sins — forgives and disregards the offenses of others." I Peter 4:8 AMP

I believe the word cover refers to the principle of replacement in the gear shift. So we would summarize by saying that, "Love is a good replacement for all sins." This is not said about any other part of the fruit of the Spirit. Here is another insight into the uniqueness of love and why we should make it our great quest in life!

A Comparison

Below is a comparison between the components/characteristics of love and the reactions in the Chain Reaction. The comparison will clearly demonstrate the absolute necessity of love in order to come out of depression. It is even more important to realize how love can prevent depression.

Look at the comparisons:

The Chain Reaction	Love
having to have my way	never selfish, does not demand its own way
anger and bitterness	not irritable, not touchy suffers long and is kind
grudge	does not hold grudges, hardly even notices when others do it wrong
self pity	never selfish hopes all things
sensitive	not irritable not touchy

It is easy to see the protection we can gain from love against these sinful reactions. Earlier I made a reference to the seemingly "epidemic" of grudge bearing among Christians.

If you decide to always replace with love and make it your great aim in life, more and more you will hardly notice when others do you wrong. When you hardly notice that others are doing you wrong, you have a good possibility of not recording a "grudge video tape." Another insight into the great protection that God provides for us in His love!

Your Love Pulse

How will you be able to know if you are a loving person? You can take your "love pulse" at any time by reviewing the 20 characteristics and see how you are doing! For that reason I challenge you to memorize the 20 characteristics.

If you want to know if you love someone then compare what goes on inside you in their presence (or even when you think about them) with love's 20 characteristics. It will be virtually impossible to escape from or prevent depression without majoring on being a loving person.

Jesus' Emphasis

Jesus certainly elevated God's love to its proper place when asked, "Master, which is the great commandment in the law? Jesus said unto him, Thou shalt love the Lord thy God with all thy heart, and with all thy soul, and with all thy mind. This is the first and great commandment. And the second is like unto it. Thou shalt love thy neighbor as thyself. On these two commandments hang all the law and the prophets."
Matthew 22:36-40 KJV

The love which produces harmonious living is not generated between people. It is from God and depends on your fellowship with him.

No Separation

"Who shall separate us from the love of Christ? Shall tribulation, or distress, or persecution, or famine, or nakedness, or peril, or sword? As it is written, For thy sake we are killed all the day long; we are accounted as sheep for the slaughter. Nay, in all these things we are more than conquerors through him that loved us. For I am persuaded, that neither death, nor life, nor angels, nor principalities, nor powers, nor things present, nor things to come, nor height, nor depth, nor any other creature, shall be able to separate us from the love of God, which is in Christ Jesus our Lord." Romans 8:35-39 KJV

Verse 35 says, who shall separate us from the love of Christ. The who is personal and refers to people, so can a person separate us from the love of Christ? The obvious answer is "no". Then there is a list of circumstances or things which cannot separate us from the love of God which is in Christ Jesus our Lord.

tribulation	life (anything that might happen to us in life)
distress	angels
persecution	principalities
famine	powers
nakedness	things present
peril	things to come
sword	height (powers of)
death	depth (powers of)
	any other creature

All the above helps us understand why verse 37 is true, "Nay in all these things we are more than conquerors through Him that loved us."

The conclusion? Nothing shall be able to separate us from the love of God which includes its 20 characteristics!

Does this include depression? I believe it does. Does the word "nothing" include a chemical imbalance? I believe it does.

After spending a lifetime studying and writing about men and events, historian-philosopher Will Durante, at age 92 , has distilled more than 2000 years of history into three simple words: "Love one another." "My final lesson of history," says Durante, "is the same as that of Jesus."

Won't you make love your aim, your great quest in life?

CHAPTER TWELVE

UNION WITH THE HOLY SPIRIT

Joe's Story — A Dramatic Turn Around

Joe is a dear Christian friend who resides in a retirement center. He is 93 years old. In the last several years I have had the opportunity to closely observe Joe and how he is experiencing the Lord each day in his walk with Him.

I have taught a Bible class at the center and Joe is a faithful attender. He is open to God's Word and learns something for himself in each lesson. It has been impressive and a challenge to see his consistent positive attitude. He reads his Bible each day and studies his devotional book. Every time I have been to visit, Joe is dressed very well. He has on a fresh shirt, tie and a sport coat or vest. As you well know, if you have visited a retirement home, this is not the description of the average person. I decided years ago if the Lord let me live beyond 90, that I would aspire to be like Joe. He has been a true inspiration.

Several months ago a close friend called to tell me that we needed to visit Joe. He was not doing well.

When we entered Joe's room I was shocked to see him sitting on the side of his bed unshaven, wearing pajamas that were soiled. Could this be Joe? What had happened in these few weeks to bring about such dramatic changes? With a pillow in one hand and a heating pad in the other, he began to complain about his back pain. His doctors were not returning his phone calls and seemed disinterested. His pharmacist friend promised to arrange for a change in his pain medication but had not done so. Joe was griping and complaining about his circumstances. His story was repeated. This continued for 30 minutes as we watched a man filled with self pity try to get comfortable. It appeared that Joe was depressed.

My friend and I wondered what we could do to help. I remembered the material I had written concerning our union with Christ and His peace and comfort. I retrieved it from my car and began to read the material to Joe.

Half way through he interrupted me to say he had not read his Bible or devotional book in six weeks. He began to confess his resentment, griping and self pity. He admitted he was depressed. I continued to read. When I finished, Joe asked me to reread certain portions especially the Proverb about pain and trouble.

"The strong spirit of a man will sustain him in bodily pain and trouble; but a weak and broken spirit who can raise up or bear."
Proverbs 18:14 AMP

We discussed the principles involved and Joe began to change before our eyes. After we had prayer Joe said, "This has given me hope. Thank you for coming."

My friend promised to arrange for another opinion about his back problem and to check with his pharmacist. The material that I left with Joe was in small print. He had trouble reading it. His tape player was broken. I promised to return the next morning with a large print version of my study, a tape player and some new tapes.

My friend and I marveled at what the Lord did in such a short time. We were amazed at the power of the Word of God. I confessed my lack of faith in what God could do and did for Joe.

The Turnaround

The next morning, only 18 hours later, I returned to the retirement home. When I opened Joe's door, there sat the Joe I remembered. He was clean shaven, dressed in clean fresh pajamas and a bathrobe. Joe said, "Come in, Sam, how are you this morning?" What a contrast from the day before. He related that he had read the material, with the aid of a magnifying glass, three times before sleeping. Then again three times earlier that morning. He did not complain about his back. The griping and self pity were gone. When I inquired about his back, he said it was better. I gave him the new large print sheets, set up the tape player and gave him the tapes.

It seemed obvious that Joe's depression had aggravated his back condition. This is common among depressed people with physical problems.

I went away for three weeks. When I returned I was anxious to see what had happened to Joe. I called my friend. He related the last three weeks to me:

1. He took Joe to a physical therapist and his back was greatly improved. The pain had decreased.
2. His emotional and spiritual state was back like the "old Joe"!
3. He had studied the material each day and was listening to the tapes for the second time.

When I visited Joe, my friend's report was accurate.

Four months later, I taught the Bible class and Joe attended. It was true he was still the "old Joe". He thanked me again and shared what the Lord did through the material and tapes. In his words they had "saved my life." What an encouragement to me. How grateful I am that the Lord let me see Him work in such a remarkable way!

A Reservoir of Faith

As a counselor I have talked with many Christians. I have shared the Word of God as it related to their problems and circumstances. Most are not sure this is adequate for their," serious complicated problem". Some take a few days or weeks and sometime months to consider if the Bible really has the answers for them. A few take the Lord at His Word and respond positively. They begin to see a consistent improvement.

Yet as I recall Joe's situation and his story I am not sure I have seen anyone respond so rapidly. As I have shared this testimony of God's faithfulness, I have been asked, "to what do you attribute Joe's immediate change?" After thinking about it I have come to a conclusion. Joe had a "reservoir of faith" upon which to draw in a time that he was depressed. As he dipped into his reservoir, he mixed his faith with the Lord's promises. As Paul Harvey would say, "And now you know the rest of the story."

Let me ask you, do you have a strong reservoir of faith? All of us have down times. Some of you have or will suffer from depression. What we will need is a reservoir to dip into to bring us back. How sad to dip the cup and hear it scrape bottom. Then looking into the cup we find little or no faith.

Almost all of us will face some type of physical breakdown in the latter years of life, so:

BE PREPARED!

Remember Noah didn't wait until the rain started to begin building the ark!

Here are two appropriate verses:

O satisfy us with Your mercy and loving kindness in the morning (now before we are older) that we may rejoice and be glad all our days.
Psalm 90:14 AMP

(Growing in grace) they shall still bring forth fruit in old age; they shall be full of sap (of spiritual vitality) and rich in the verdure (of trust, love and contentment); (They are living memorials) to show that the Lord is upright and faithful to His promises; He is my rock, and there is no unrighteousness in Him. Psalm 92:14 & 15 AMP

Union of the Human Spirit With the Holy Spirit

The following information is a study that I worked on for several years. This is what I shared with Joe.

The purpose of this study is to explore the means by which a Christian can experience God's peace and comfort (and other parts of the fruit of the Spirit) in the presence of difficult circumstances, tribulation and even bodily pain. This would include abnormal changes in all of the body's functions. These changes could be a chemical imbalance, elevated blood pressure, colitis, cancer, ulcers, and others. Many people become depressed because of their reactions to their physical problems. This is what happened to Joe.

Once he was free of his depression, he still had his back pain. Yet when he placed his faith in God and His promises, he was able to experience the Lord's love, joy, comfort and peace as he lived with his pain.

It is for this reason I have included the study in this book about depression. If you have or should have some kind of physical breakdown, please don't make yourself an exception and fail to take advantage of what God offers you. The study follows a logical pattern of thoughts and facts.

First, the need to establish on the basis of scripture the union of the human spirit with the Holy Spirit.

Second, the distinction between the peace *of* God and the peace *from* God and what is unique about His peace.

Third, the fact that all of this is to be appropriated by faith.

I have selected four words found in scripture that denote union. They are:

1. Make alive with or quicken
2. Yoke
3. Baptize
4. Partakers

Make Alive With or Quicken

Life - ZOE - ZOO
Make alive - ZOOPOIEO
Make alive with - SUNZOOPOIEO = quicken
These Greek words build one on the other to form the English word.

....He made us alive together ... in union with Christ. He gave us the very life of Christ Himself, the same new life. Ephesians 2:5 AMP

... hath quickened us together with Christ. Ephesians 2:5 KJV

.... brought to life together with Christ. Col. 2:13 KJV

.... hath he quickened together with Him. Col. 2:13 AMP

.... It is the Spirit that gives life. John 6:63 AMP

In conclusion, be strong in the Lord — be empowered through your union with Him; draw your strength from Him — that strength which His (boundless) might provides. Ephesians 6:10 AMP

"Someone has said, union with Jesus is so strong, that nothing can break it. Communion with Jesus is so fragile that the slightest sin can break it." Kenneth Wuest

Yoke

Definition: Serving to couple two things together, a submission to authority.

Take my yoke upon you, and learn of me; for I am meek and lowly in heart: and ye shall find rest unto your souls. For my yoke is easy, and my burden is light. Matt.11:29-30 KJV

Christ's yoke is not simply imparted by Him but is shared with Him.

Listed below are all the benefits as stated in the Amplified Bible from the same passages:

Take my yoke upon you, and learn of Me:
1.   Gentle (meek)
2.   Humble (lowly)
3.   Find rest — relief, ease, and refreshment, recreation, blessed quiet — for your souls
4.   Wholesome — useful — good
5.   Not harsh, hard, sharp, or pressing
6.   Comfortable
7.   Gracious
8.   Pleasant
9.   Light
10. Easy to be borne

Baptize

The Greek word for baptize is BAPTIZO — "The introduction or placing of a person or thing into a new environment or into union with something else so as to alter its condition or its relationship to its previous environment or condition."

"Its usage in Romans chapter 6: It refers to the act of God reducing a believing sinner into vital union with Jesus Christ..." Kenneth Wuest

Partakers

.....by which have been given to us exceedingly great and precious promises, that through these you may be partakers of the divine nature.
II Peter 1:4(b) KJV

Websters first dictionary: One who has or takes a part, share or portion in common with others; a sharer; a participant.

Vines— (a noun) denoting a companion, partner; signifying having in common.

.... partakers of His holiness   Heb.12:10(b) KJV

Other verses and quotes that denote union:

We were buried therefore with Him by the baptism into death, so that just as Christ was raised from the dead by the glorious (power) of the Father, so we too might live and behave in newness of life. Romans 6:4 AMP

The verb SUNPHUO in Romans 6:5 means: "to grow up together with" It speaks of a living, vital union of two individuals growing up together.

--- "we have become permanently united with Him with respect to the likeness of His resurrection." Kenneth Wuest

But the person who is united to the Lord becomes one Spirit with Him.
        I Corinthians 6:17 AMP

At that time — when that day comes— you will know (for yourselves) that I am in My Father, and you (are) in Me, and I (am) in you.
        John 14:20 AMP

The Spirit of truth... He lives with you (constantly) and will be in you.
        John 14:17 AMP

"The spirit-nature in the natural man is dead toward God. It must have a Divine quickening. It is in that quickened spirit-nature that the Holy Spirit dwells." Evan Hopkins

"It is the coming of the Holy Spirit *into* the human spirit which constitutes that spiritual new birth by which we may be born into the family of God and become His children, and it is the presence of the Holy Spirit *within* the human spirit which constitutes the seal God sets upon this new relationship." Major Ian Thomas

God's Peace

But the fruit *of* the Spirit is, love, joy, peace, ... Gal. 5:21(a) AMP

Notice that it is the fruit of the Spirit not from the Spirit.

Notice also that obtaining God's peace, is something between you and God and has nothing to do with people.

Peace is something the Spirit imparts to us as a part of His being. It is not something He gives to us apart from Himself. To experience this

peace, that Jesus talked about and promised, it is necessary that the Holy Spirit not only be in our lives but in control.
For He is (Himself) our peace ... Eph. 2:14(a) AMP

To proclaim to the Gentiles the unending (boundless, fathomless, incalculable and exhaustless) riches *of* Christ — wealth which no human being could have searched out. Eph. 3:8(b) AMP

And God's peace (be yours, that tranquil state of a soul assured of its salvation through Christ, and so fearing nothing from God and content with its earthly lot whatever sort that is, that peace) which transcends all understanding shall garrison and mount guard over your hearts and minds in Christ Jesus. Phil.4:7 AMP

Peace of God ... rule (act as umpire continually) in your hearts — deciding and settling with finality all questions that arise in your minds — (in that peaceful state) to which (as members) of Christ's one body) you were also called (to live). Col. 3:15 AMP

So beloved since you are expecting these things, be eager to be found by Him (at His coming) without spot or blemish, and at peace— in serene confidence, free from fears and agitating passions and moral conflicts.
II Peter 3:14 AMP

Now may the Lord of peace Himself grant you His peace ... at all times and in all ways — under all circumstances and conditions, whatever comes. II Thes. 3:16 AMP

May the God of peace be with you all! Romans 15:33 AMP

You will guard him and keep him in perfect and constant peace whose mind (both its inclination and its character) is stayed on You, because he commits himself to You, leans on You and hopes confidently in You.
Isaiah 26:3 AMP

Exclaiming, would that you had known personally even at least in this your day, the things that make for peace (for freedom from all the distresses that are experienced as a result of sin, and upon which your peace, that is, your security, safety, prosperity, and happiness depends)!

But now they are hidden from your eyes. Luke 19:42 AMP

This your day denotes present tense. Notice that distresses are a result of sin. Therefore it is vital that we constantly keep our heart and confess our sin as soon as we are aware of it.

Luke 19:38 Reads virtually the same as verse 42 but is future tense.

Peace I leave with you; My own peace I now give and bequeath to you. Not as the world gives do I give to you. Do not let your heart be troubled, neither let it be afraid — stop allowing yourselves to be agitated and disturbed; and do not permit yourselves to be fearful and intimidated and cowardly and unsettled. John 14:27 AMP

.....But the mind of the (Holy) Spirit is life and soul — peace (both now and forever). Romans 8:6(b) AMP

Experiencing God's peace is one of the evidences that we are walking in the Spirit. In Isaiah 32:17, God promises that the work of righteousness (choosing to do what is right) shall be peace and the effect of righteousness quietness and assurance forever. KJV
This is not a promise that our days won't contain trouble. It says our hearts need not be troubled in the midst of those troublesome days.

FAITH

"Place your confidence in His ability to do just what He says He will do. (Philippian jailer) A definite taking of one's self out of one's keeping and entrusting one's self into the keeping of the Lord Jesus." Kenneth Wuest

In Whom, because of our *faith* in Him, we dare to have the boldness (courage and confidence) of free access, and unreserved approach to God with freedom and without fear. Ephesians 3:12 AMP

.....but we are of those who believe — who cleave to and trust in and rely on God through Jesus Christ, the Messiah — and by faith preserve the soul. Hebrews 10:39(b) AMP (the soul is the mind, emotions and will.)

"All that I have seen, teaches me to trust the Creator for all I have not seen." Emerson

Vines -- Firm persuasion, a conviction based upon hearing.
    a. trust
    b. trustworthiness
       1. A firm conviction, producing a full
          acknowledgement of God's revelation or truth.
       2. A personal surrender to Him.
       3. A conduct inspired by such surrender.

The following definition of faith in Webster's Original Dictionary is excellent.

Evangelical, justifying, or saving faith, is the assent of the mind to the truth of divine revelation, on the authority of God's testimony, accompanied with a cordial assent of the will or approbation of the heart; an entire confidence or trust in God's character and declarations, and in the character and doctrines of Christ, with an unreserved surrender of the will to his guidance, and dependence on his merits for salvation. In other words, that firm belief of God's testimony, and of the truth of the gospel, which influences the will, and leads to an entire reliance on Christ for salvation.

Conclusions

In order to tie all this together, we have seen that the human spirit is in union with the Holy Spirit in the life of the believer. We also saw that the peace the world gives is not the same as that which the Holy Spirit gives. The Living Bible says the world's peace is fragile.

God's peace is also described as without understanding. (Philippians 4:7) Modern science has been able to discover the areas of the brain where the "sense of well being" is located. There are several neuro chemicals that are critical in maintaining a sense of well being. These chemicals have been isolated and through analysis of body fluids, it can be determined whether or not they are at the proper levels. So now there are prescription drugs that can help in maintaining the proper balance of those chemicals.

All of this demonstrates that man has come to understand not only where the center of "well being" resides, but through the use of certain drugs that "well being" can be maintained. It seems in the literature that the word "peace" is avoided. However, I feel that this is their attempt to bring peace to the troubled patient. One of the verses that was quoted stated that the peace of God is without understanding. So this peace would have to be different from what modern science has uncovered — for it is understandable!

In reading the literature about psychiatric drugs, it is interesting to see the effects of their use in treating mental disorders. Here is a list of the effects: quiet the symptoms, counteract depression, lessen highs and lows, counteract sense of doom and reduce compulsions. Notice the absence of terms like: removal, eliminate, eradicate and cure.

An Avenue

Because the Bible states that the fruit of the Spirit is available under any circumstances or conditions, there must be an "avenue" of experiencing God's peace that does not depend on the normal channels.

Since the human spirit is in union with the Holy Spirit in the believer, there must be a means of the experiencing of peace that flows directly from the person of the Holy Spirit to the human spirit. The quoted verses state that nothing can separate us from the Holy Spirit and His peace. Therefore, His peace is not dependent on the absence of certain physical conditions which we are normally told (even by well meaning Christians) would block the ability to have His peace.

Two great promises in the Proverbs:
The strong spirit of a man will sustain him in bodily pain and trouble, but a weak and broken spirit who can raise up or bear? Proverbs 18:14 AMP
A calm and undisturbed mind and heart are the life and health of the body, but envy, jealousy and wrath are as rottenness to the bones.
Proverbs 14:30 AMP

Grace (favor and spiritual blessing) to you and (heart) peace from God our Father and the Lord Jesus Christ, the Messiah, the Anointed One. Blessed (be) the God and Father of our Lord Jesus Christ, the Father of sympathy (pity and mercies) and the God (who is the source) of every consolation and comfort and encouragement : Who consoles and comforts and encourages us in every trouble (calamity and affliction), so that we may also be able to console (comfort and encourage) those who are in any kind of trouble or distress, with the consolation (comfort and encouragement) with which we ourselves are consoled and comforted and encouraged by God. II Corinthians 1:2-4 AMP

The Lord is my strength, my personal bravery and my invincible army; He makes my feet like hinds' feet, and will make me to walk not to stand still in terror but to walk and make (spiritual) progress upon my high places (of trouble, suffering or responsibility)!! Habakkuk 3:19 AMP

References used in this chapter:
Evan Hopkins, The Law of Liberty in the Spiritual Life
        (Philadelphia, The Sunday School Times, 1960)
Kenneth S.Wuest, Word Studies, Golden Nuggets from the Greek
        New Testament (Grand Rapids, MI, Wm.B.Erdmans Publishing
        Co., 1962)
W.E. Vine, An Expository Dictionary of New Testament Words
        (Westwood, NJ, Fleming H.Revell Company, 1966)
Major Ian Thomas, If I Perish,I Perish (Great Britian,Capernwray
        Press, 1991)
Websters Original Dictionary printed in 1828.

13

CLOSING SUMMARY

Science Arrives — Four Thousand Years Late

Several years ago an article appeared in a local newspaper entitled, "Doctors finding religion improves health." It began, "Maybe doctors should write go to church weekly on their prescription pads. Evidence is growing that religion can be good medicine."

The author said that research shows benefits of religion on dealing with drug abuse, alcoholism, depression, cancer, high blood pressure and heart disease.

Preliminary results show that people who attend church are both physically healthier and less depressed. The article continued to say it is not clear just how religion makes people healthier, although theories abound. At least one piece of research raises the possibility that divine intervention is the answer. Taking part in prayer and ritual may lower harmful stress hormones in the body such as adrenaline.

Dr. Herbert Benson of Harvard Medical School stated, "Studies have shown this kind of stress reduction can reduce high blood pressure, chronic pain, insomnia, anxiety, infertility and pre-menstrual syndrome, among other things." The article ended with his comment, "Prayer is good for you."

He and others recommended that doctors take religion more seriously as a way of keeping people healthy. As we read articles like this, it becomes obvious that there is at least one book these researchers have not read!

A Logical Conclusion

In closing, we will attempt to tie all of this together so that we can better understand how to respond to the everyday situations of life. The logical steps are:

1. You will recall in Galatians 5: 21-23, that God's love, joy and peace are the fruit of the Holy Spirit. It is not unusual to place your conditions or circumstances in the verse in order to make you an exception. For example: The fruit of the Spirit (unless my marriage is bad or I have an illness or I am in chronic pain or I have a chemical imbalance) is love, joy, peace, longsuffering, etc. Do you have an "unless"? Possibly you would like to fill in the blank. The fruit of the Spirit (unless _____) is love, joy, peace, longsuffering, etc.

2. In chapter twelve I documented the fact that, in the Christian, The Holy Spirit is in union with the human spirit. This explains the unique passage of the fruit of the Spirit to the human spirit. When this occurs, you begin to experience God's love, joy, peace, longsuffering, etc.

3. If you are not experiencing the fruit of the Spirit, what does the Bible say prevents this experience ? This occurs when fellowship with the Lord is broken. What breaks this fellowship ? SIN! There is an appropriate warning in Ephesians 4: 30, "And grieve not the Holy Spirit of God, whereby ye are sealed unto the day of redemption." This warning against grieving the Holy Spirit falls in the con text of verses 25 through 31. The list of actions or reactions in those verses give a description of someone walking in disobedience or in unconfessed sin. Any one of them is capable of breaking fellowship with the Lord.

4. If sin blocks experiencing the fruit of the Spirit and you desire to restore that experience, where should your focus be ? Obviously you should examine your life for any unconfessed sin. Let me warn you that this approach is rarely considered. That is why I stated earlier that this book would take a unique approach. If you examine your life and God convicts you of any unconfessed sin, then you need to shift gears. By confessing your sin you will go from reverse to neutral. Your sin is gone because God has cleansed you according to His promise in I John 1:9 . In order to go from neutral to forward, you need to ask God to fill you with the Holy Spirit. Also ask Him for any specific parts of the fruit of the Spirit that you deem necessary. Remember to always start with love! Once you

are in forward, you are again walking in the Spirit. It is in forward gear, as you walk in the Spirit, that you will have protection from falling back into reverse . This is because of God's promise in Galatians 5:16, "This I say then, Walk in the Spirit, and ye shall not fulfill the lust (the desires) of the flesh." KJV

A Short Review of the Chain Reaction

As we go through life, it is our natural tendency to want to have our own way and to become angry if we do not get it. If left alone, anger, which is an acute feeling, will turn into bitterness or resentment. We believe that bitterness is the chronic form of anger. If we fail to eliminate this bitterness, we will be troubled by it. (Heb. 12:15) One of the best ways to relieve this troubled spirit, is to recall the incident that resulted in bitterness. This is called a grudge. By reviewing the incident, we justify, defend and rationalize our bitterness and temporary relief is provided. The relief is only temporary because each time we recall the incident we are "fertilizing the root of bitterness." Grudge-bearing leads to self-pity. People who feel sorry for themselves become sensitive. Sensitive people have to have their own way more than nonsensitive people. It is easier to "set them off" and anger reappears. Another cycle through the chain reaction has begun.

Once this first reaction in the chain occurs, it will lead to and through the other reactions. Unless the chain of reactions is interrupted, the initial cycle and others will begin to accumulate.

There may be some difficulty in identifying with the Chain Reaction. The difficulty comes from one or more of the following reasons:

1. Reactions can be mild and go unnoticed.
2. The subtle way in which they occur may be deceiving.
3. A long standing habit of allowing reactions to accumulate and not doing anything about it or not knowing what to do.
4. The tendency to justify and rationalize reactions.
5. A repressor may feel he does not need to deal with these reactions until and unless they are expressed.

Early Recognition

The application of this Chain Reaction in our lives should not be dismissed, because it occurs in all of us. Even though I have used it in relation to depression, it is obvious that the reactions build up inside us long before we become depressed. Reactions should be prayerfully examined the next time something does not go as desired. Those who have been willing to identify and deal with their sinful reactions (responses) have found it to be a life-changing experience! It is possible not to feel the impact of these reactions and cycles until they begin to accumulate.

It is much healthier, spiritually and emotionally, to interrupt the chain before you begin to feel the impact. People who wait for a build-up to occur before they deal with it, tend to go from one crisis, or breakdown, to another. Over a period of years the crisis, or breakdown, tends to occur closer and closer together. The onset of depression will occur when the number of cyclings exceeds a person's tolerance. The absence of depression does not mean the Chain Reaction does not apply. The Chain Reaction applies to everyone and unchecked, will eventually result in depression.

Brief Review of the Four Questions

Due to our concern about and interest in depression, I have sought to study it thoroughly. In concluding the book, I trust you have found answers to the four questions that were listed in the beginning.
1. What is depression?
2. How do you become depressed?
3. How can you be free of depression?
4. How can you prevent depression?

The answer to the first question:
Basically depression is the result of the accumulation of negative responses. These responses occur inside of us and may be expressed or repressed or both. The characteristics or symptoms are caused or directly related to these negative responses.

The answer to the second question:
A cycle through the Chain Reaction occurs when unconfessed anger, bitterness, grudges and self-pity goes uninterrupted. Chapters three through seven dealt with each of the parts that make up the Chain Reaction. Each person has a tolerance of the number of cycles before they become depressed. When the tolerance is exceeded, depression begins to set in.

The answer to the third question:
Since all of the parts of the Chain Reaction are sinful, they need to be confessed. Repentance is also necessary. The application of the gear shift principle allows cleansing and the opportunity to walk in the Spirit.

The answer to the fourth question:
Prevention comes through a strong commitment to interrupt the Chain Reaction and break the cycle by shifting gears and walking in the Spirit. As you walk in the Spirit remember to make love, "your aim, your great quest in life." In so doing there will be no accumulation of cycles to lead to depression.

The chapter on love needs to be reviewed often. God's love as we walk in the Spirit, is our great protector against yielding to temptation and responding sinfully. Again let me challenge you to memorize the twenty characteristics as found in I Cor.13:4-8(a). (listed in chapter eleven)

There is reality in the spiritual realm just as there is in the physical realm. Jesus Christ through the Holy Spirit lives in us! Our union with Christ exists as the Holy Spirit is in vital union with our human spirit. The tremendous benefits of that union were explained in chapter twelve.

Years ago I heard a statement that became very important to me. It is:

SIMPLICITY IS THE ESSENCE OF ALL THINGS PROFOUND

The Biblical principles and verses contained in this book are very simple in their message and application. And because of that they are often rejected. However if you believe the above statement, then you will have to conclude that because of their simplicity, they are profound. God desires that you allow Him to use them in order to have a profound effect in your life. Will you let Him?

As stated earlier, one out of every seven Americans will suffer depression to the point that counseling will be sought. We need not become one of the one-in-seven. As Christians, we can trust God and His promises by practicing these Biblical principles and be free of and avoid depression.

Sharing

If you know someone who is depressed or is frequently bothered by depression, please consider sharing this book with them. As you do ask them to prayerfully consider this Biblical approach. Challenge them to give the Lord a try. He is faithful!!

The last two pages have full page diagrams of the Chain Reaction and the gear shift. Please feel free to photocopy them for your personal use or in order to help someone else.

Shifting Gears

Galatians 5:16

Replace specifically

Matthew 12:43-45

I John 1:9

F

N

R

Beware — There is no prevention in neutral!

Chain Reaction

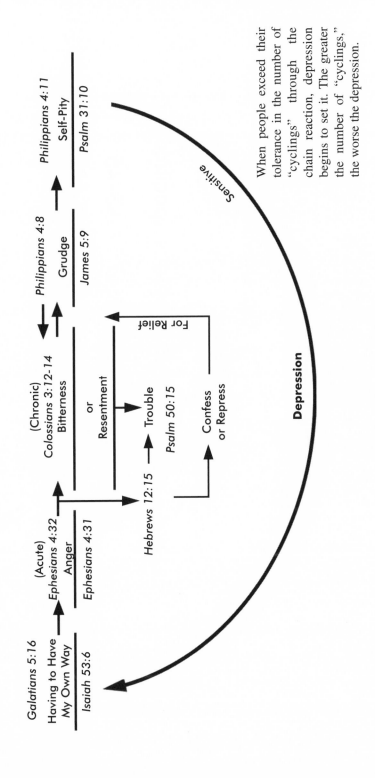

Galatians 5:16
Having to Have
My Own Way

Isaiah 53:6

(Acute)
Ephesians 4:32
Anger

Ephesians 4:31

Hebrews 12:15 → Trouble

Psalm 50:15

Confess
or Repress

(Chronic)
Colossians 3:12-14
Bitterness

or
Resentment

For Relief

Philippians 4:8
Grudge

James 5:9

Philippians 4:11
Self-Pity

Psalm 31:10

Sensitive

Depression

When people exceed their tolerance in the number of "cyclings" through the chain reaction, depression begins to set it. The greater the number of "cyclings," the worse the depression.